ME AND OUR KID

ME AND OUR KID

THE STORY OF TWO BIRMINGHAM WAR BABIES

Malcolm Cox

BREWIN BOOKS

First published by
Brewin Books Ltd, 56 Alcester Road,
Studley, Warwickshire B80 7LG in 2019
www.brewinbooks.com

© Malcolm Cox 2019

All rights reserved.

ISBN: 978-1-85858-703-5

The moral right of the author has been asserted.

A Cataloguing in Publication Record
for this title is available from the British Library.

Typeset in Haarlemmer MT Std
Printed in Great Britain by
4edge Ltd.

Contents

Preface	vii
Chapter One	1
Chapter Two	9
Chapter Three	16
Chapter Four	20
Chapter Five	26
Chapter Six	30
Chapter Seven	34
Chapter Eight	40
Chapter Nine	47
Chapter Ten	54
Chapter Eleven	63
Chapter Twelve	71
Appendix	72

Preface

I presented a record of our early years to my elder brother David – Our Kid – on his 60th birthday.

The anecdotes in my story are dedicated particularly to the memory of our jailors, inquisitors and mentors, Ada and Alfred Cox, our loving Mom and Dad, and, of course, to Our Kid. These are the certain memories and moments in life that as you get older you treasure. They are written as a personal account of the joys and misfortunes of me and Our Kid when we were two little urchins with the backside hanging out of our trousers (sorry Mom), related mainly as remembered, in no special order. It is a trip down memory lane. I laughed whilst writing some of it and cried at others, but I needed to put it all down on paper.

These are followed by some highlights of how we two urchins fared later: what has happened to us over the course of the rest of our lives. And to finish: an appendix giving our family tree, our relatives and a few pics from our family album.

We are both now in our 70s. After all these years, the relationship we still share is as strong as two siblings could have.

Malcolm

*In memory of
our Mom and Dad*

Chapter One

Brung up in Hockley...

Me and Our Kid were brought up in Birmingham, in an area called Hockley. We lived in a terrace house and our street was called Wellesley Street. David was born 7th May 1941 and I was born 2nd December 1943. Dad worked for the railway at the goods depot in Curzon Street in Birmingham. His job was to deliver goods from there around the Birmingham area, first on a horse and cart and then by a variety of lorries, his first being the three-wheel Scammell.

Mom was a typical mom, who wore what seemed to be standard Mom issue at the time: wrap-around pinnie, Stephanie Bowman corsets and a turban. Oh! – and not forgetting the slippers with pom-poms on the front. She was chief jailor in our house. When you were grounded, you were grounded, usually with bread and water for the duration of your stay in jail (the back bedroom).

Our house was typical of the other terrace houses in Wellesley Street: your Mom scrubbed the front door step every morning and swept your part of the street. We were not allowed to play in the front room and Dad polished the lino around the rug every Sunday morning. Once a month the man who painted the house numbers appeared in his trilby and brown Mac with his little pot of white paint and paint brush and did your numbers – ours was 122. In our early years, the only meat the local butcher sold was rabbit, but then chicken appeared which we had every Sunday, followed by rice pudding covered in nutmeg. The shout of "baggy the skin!" could be heard up the street but Our Kid always seemed to win this valuable prize.

A born leader of our gang emerges...

It was apparent from very early on in life that Our Kid was born to be a leader of men. You knew you could trust him implicitly, like when he told me to dive off the air raid shelter onto the brick yard below, resulting in me being scarred for life. I still have the imprint of a perfect set of four-year-old child's teeth in my lower lip!

Mom and Dad.

Chapter One

He would not bend under interrogation from the jailors, even when he left me tied to a lamp post (totem pole) in the dark on a bomb-peck (a place flattened by the Germans in the Second World War). It was six hours before he deigned to tell Mom and Dad where he'd left me, and who finally found this screaming cowboy terrified in the dark.

Obviously with such drive and magnetism the question of who would be gang leader was never in doubt.

The street was constructed in blocks of terrace houses with what were charmingly termed 'avenues' in between, with further terrace houses running off the avenue. The gang, therefore, was local to half a block each side of and including the avenue. Our avenue was called Ruckley Avenue and this was our patch.

Our gang consisted of the following members: Brian Reeves, Johnny Bullus, Johnny Walsh and Our Kid. These were the senior members, who tolerated Gordon Stanley, Stuart Reeves and me as juniors. Under sufferance, females (sisters) were included in the gang, if they hadn't been our mums all said we couldn't go out to fight the Sheriff of Nottingham or help Lash Larue. Carol Reeves, Pamela Walsh, Patti Walsh and Valerie Black were the female contingent of the gang.

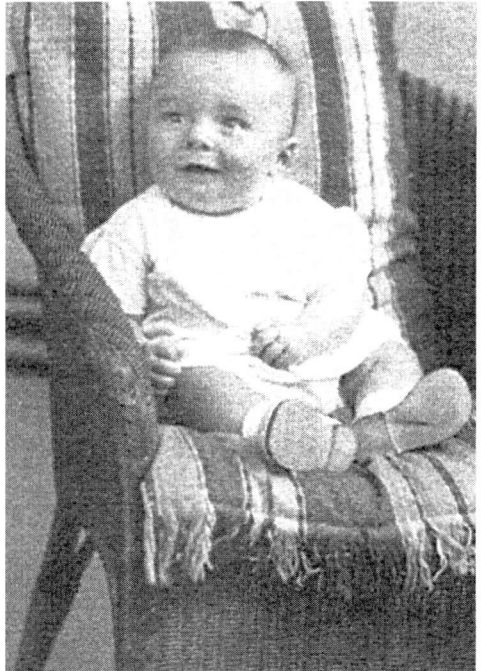
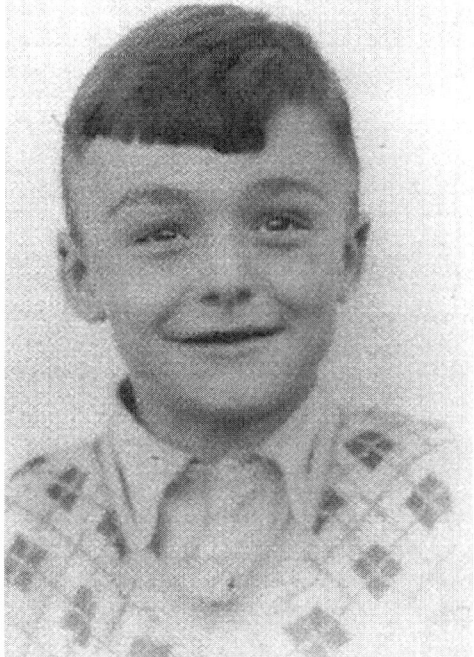

Our Kid.

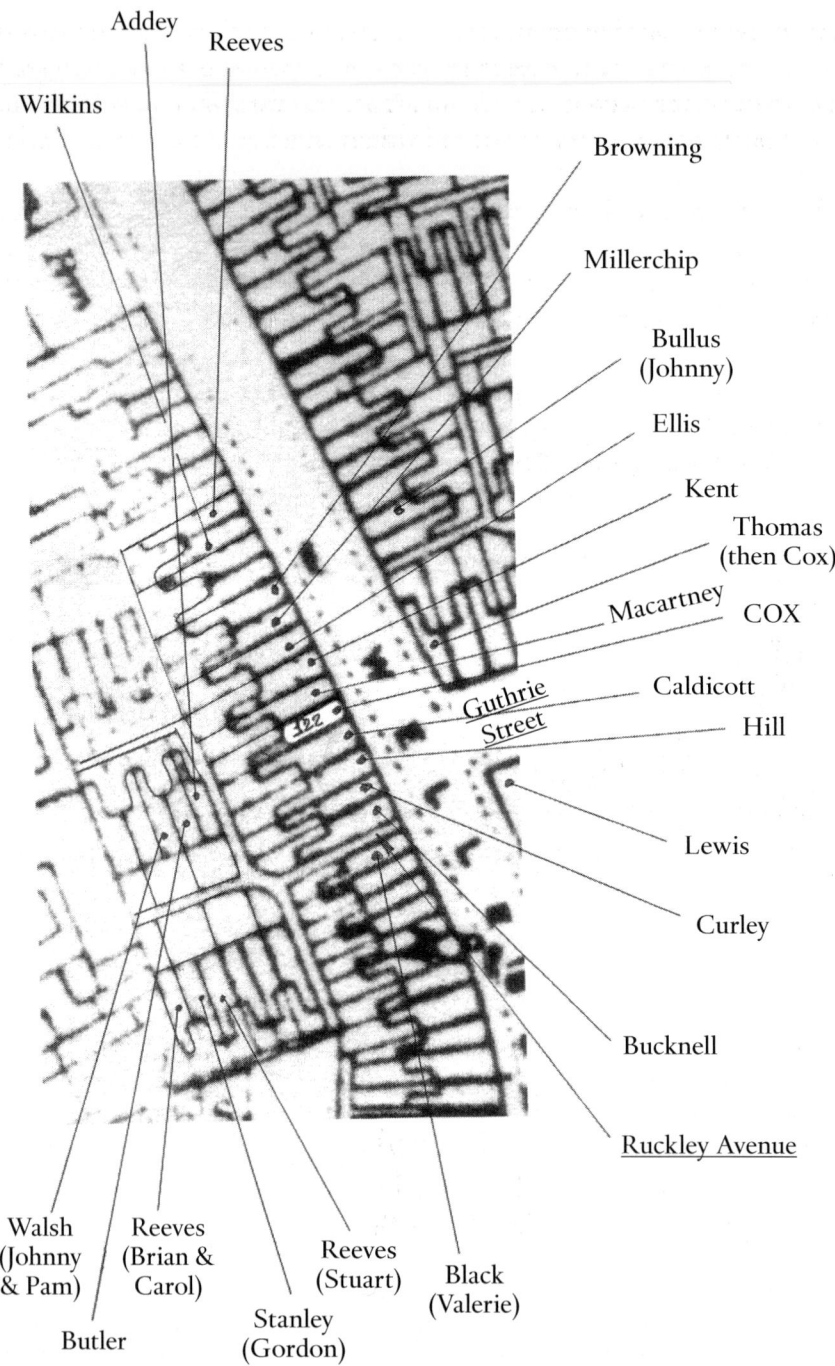

Our Street, avenue, neighbours and gang members.

Chapter One

For reasons that are not quite clear to me, me and Our Kid went to different schools. Our Kid went to a school up the road called Anglesey Street Junior School and I went to a school called Burbury Street Junior School down the road. This turned out to be a fairly good idea as it restricted the terror Our Kid could inflict on me.

It was always a love-hate relationship between us, he was forced (by our Mom) to drag me around with him. I was totally aware of this and knew he'd get rid of me at the first opportunity, but this aside we loved each other as brothers should and got on with life in what was an austere Britain just after the Second World War.

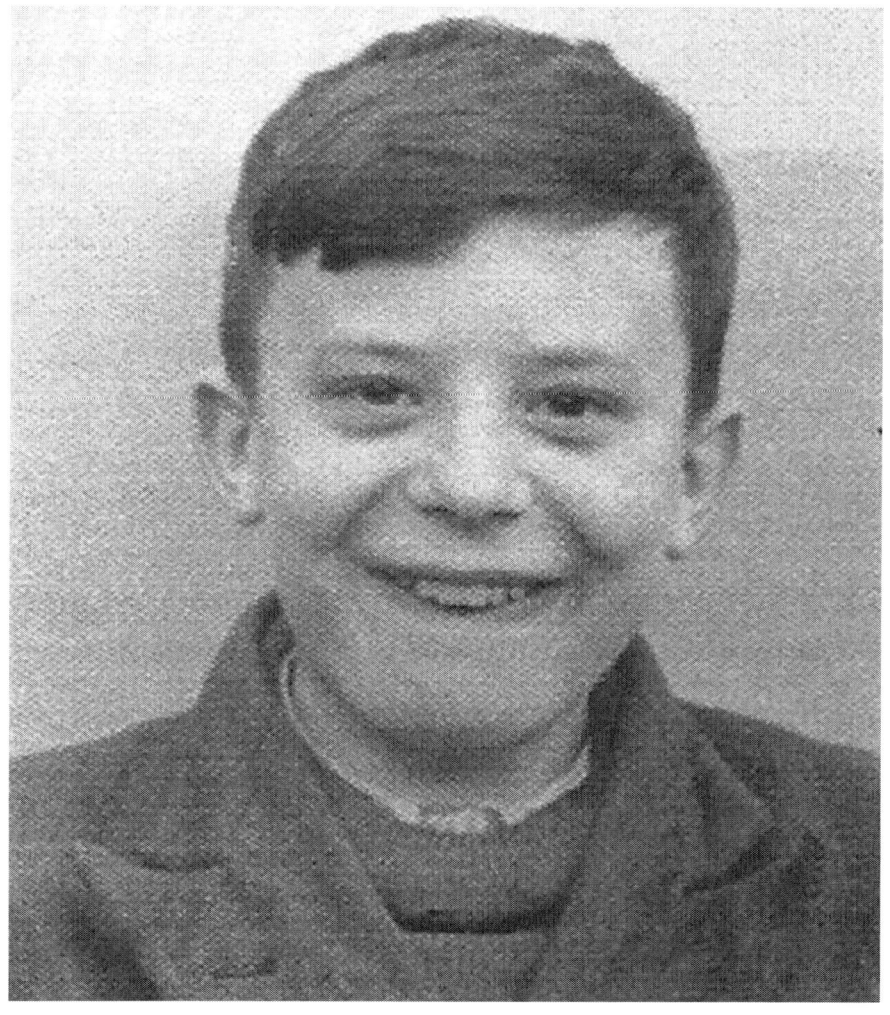

Me, junior member of our gang.

It was obvious from an early age Our Kid knew no fear. No cuddly toy for him, oh no! A shilling's worth of nails and a hammer please, with which he'd go out in the back yard and promptly nail into the paling fence between us and old Mrs. Caldicott next door. That fence was still standing totally solid with nails when I left the place when I was twenty-one.

His time with his hammer was, however, short. Our Mom had obtained a council grant to have the old cast iron grate removed and replaced with one of those new lovely posh tiled ones. From the tale my Dad told me it lasted about a week before Our Kid decided to restyle it with, you've guessed it, his hammer. Result – toy confiscated. Our Kid led screaming to jail!

Knitted swimming trunks...

Because everything was on ration after the war, all our gloves, socks, balaclavas and pullovers were knitted.

Our Kid and Me in our woolly swimming trunks with cousin Dorothy.

Chapter One

The pullover doubled as swimming trunks, the conversion from one to the other was as follows: your mom sewed the neck up, the arms would become leg holes, extra strong elastic put around the waist and hey presto! A pair of swimming trunks!

Of course, things not made for a specific purpose have their drawbacks, of which you were completely unaware until you actually got into the water. There was a heavy sensation in your crotch area when you were swimming, and when you came out of the water you realised that you had brought half the swimming baths with you, which hung in the delicate area like a sack of potatoes!

Still, the gang were all in the same boat, except Gordon Stanley whose dad earned more money than the rest of our dads: he had a proper pair of trunks which left his delicate area waterless. Needless to say he was banned from entering the Olympics at Handsworth Municipal Baths!

I reckon that if David Wilkie had trained in a pair of my Mom's swimming trunks he'd have got more medals than Mark Spitz!

Our snow fort disaster...

When you look back to when you were a lad, you seem to remember it never rained during the school holidays and you always had three foot of snow in the winter. Of course, this is just fond memories of days gone by.

But one winter I remember was a cracker, we actually had three foot of snow and all the kids thought this was great!

Our Kid summoned the gang and said we would build a fort in the entry (avenue). We soon warmed to our task and started forming igloo type blocks. The fort was built in no time at all including ramparts, slit holes for the arrows and an arch over the door. It was great fighting imaginary battles for the rest of the day!

We agreed to meet next morning to see off the rest of the Vikings before we had any errands to do for our moms.

What we hadn't taken into account was the size of our fort and the fact that it would start freezing as soon as the sun went down.

The first sign of trouble was first thing in the morning when we were greeted with a cuff around the ear hole off our Mom as we came downstairs, being accused of maiming the old age pensioner who lived in the first house up the avenue. Apparently, he had walked into our fort on the way back from the pub, because the fort happened to be in the way of his gate! With no breakfast we were all sent out with shovels, spades, hammers etc. to knock down our beloved fort. I'm sure Great Britain was raped and pillaged that day, but I wasn't too bothered because my bottom was too sore to care!

Gordon's posh sledge crash...

We also did a lot of sledging that winter on a sledge of the home-made variety lovingly made by our dads, but Gordon Stanley turned up with this beautiful, polished wood, all singing and dancing, professionally manufactured one. It even had a steering wheel.

Our Kid said "let's go down to Handsworth Park and try it out on the cricket slopes", which were covered in good snow. Now these slopes surrounded the cricket pitch and were pretty steep, ending in a sheer drop and whilst the robust sledge our Dad had built easily stood up to flying off into space with four kids on board, doubt was raised about the vulnerability of Gordon's sledge. Gang leader dismissed our misgivings out of hand and duly organised the four man bob run. We shot off into space as usual but on landing finished up with a pile of firewood wrapped around us. Poor Gordon.

Me and Our Kid then drew straws on who was going to tell Mom, you can guess who lost. I'm sure I have one ear thicker than the other thanks to Our Kid and my mother's right hook.

Our Kid, Johnny Bullus and Johnny Walsh.

Chapter Two

Plenty of bananas and fish...

Working on the railway, our dad used to deliver goods to all the wholesale markets in Birmingham City Centre.

When he delivered to the banana warehouse on a Monday he was always given a hand of bananas and when he went to the fish warehouse on a Friday he was given a box of wet plaice. Dad used to hand these over to Mom who would

Dad receiving a driver's safety award.

share them with the neighbours, so we all got fresh fruit and fish, at a time when rationing after the War was still in force. At the time we kids thought nothing of it, but looking back it showed a total lack of selfishness on our parents' part in what were hard times. Our neighbours in return used to give Mom any bread they had left over, with which she proceeded to make bread pudding – for years we had that as our elevenses at school. It always felt like you'd eaten a brick, but it kept us from hunger for hours.

Our dad and our soapbox cart...

All the gangs had soapbox carts and we were no exception. Now, to the uninitiated, a soapbox cart is a schoolboy's means of transport. It consisted of a long plank of wood to which were attached two large pram wheels at the back and two small pram wheels at the front. The front ones swivelled to give steerage via a rope attached to the axle just behind the wheels. A wooden box (soapbox) was positioned behind the back wheels with the front portion removed to make a seat.

The vehicle had a team, one pusher/back brake man (hands) and one driver who steered the cart and applied the front brake (shoes). A good team was not long in training, as shoes and hands did not come cheap!

Obviously the prime position in the team was the driver, but being as Our Kid was older and bigger than me, it was obvious who had to be the pusher in our team.

After the War all streets had what we termed 'pig bins'. These were dustbins put at strategic points down the street for our mothers to put all the household edible waste in, such as stale bread, potato peelings, cabbage stalks etc. These were emptied by the pig bin men and this waste was taken to farmers to feed their livestock.

During the summer these bins used to hum with flies around rotting vegetables. Our delight used to be to come charging down our street on our soapbox cart and just clip the bin with it causing the bin to spin out of control, giving us time to get away before it fell over and spewed its contents on the pavement!

This was good fun until one day we did not time our run to our usual perfection and collided with the bins just below the corner paper shop owned by a formidable dragon called Mrs. Lewis.

Before we could extricate ourselves from the ensuing debris, Mrs. Lewis shot out immediately from behind the counter in the shop, charged down the road like an Olympian and belted Our Kid around the head with the *Sports Argos* and confiscated the cart!

We stupidly complained to our Mom who promptly said Mrs. Lewis was right to confiscate our Ferrari and we got belted again for misbehaving!

I never can remember what happened to that cart, but thankfully Gordon Stanley (the lad with the rich dad) had a spare cart so we whipped his and carried on with our reign of terror! Thankfully Gordon bore no grudge for he, like myself, being a younger member of the gang, was a close mate.

Bonfire night, the coffin wood and bangers...

Bonfire night and the lead up to it was always an exciting and anxious time. The various gangs of kids would go round with their soap carts or old prams looking for combustible materials. Our favourite spot was Hodgsons the funeral directors and, you've guessed it, coffin wood. Coffin wood was a slow burner and therefore a must on your fire. Now this is where the anxious bit comes in because the wood was in short supply so you were always worried about marauding gangs creeping under cover of darkness and stealing your coffin wood!

One year the Wilkins gang from the next avenue stole some of our prized bonfire material on November 5th itself so it was decided to sneak up on their bonfire on the night and lob a few bangers at them. This turned out to be a bad move, for just as we were throwing a monumental Gordon Stanley one penny 'Thunderclap' (he was the only one who could afford them) into the fire, Frank Wilkins, father of Roy and Barry, charged at us with a lighted piece of wood. This put us off our aim so that the banger exploded in the vicinity of Frank Wilkins' legs resulting in the blowing away of half a trouser leg. This was reported back to Mom, result, into jail!

Another year Our Kid had this bright idea of gathering together all the dud fireworks from the night before and making one large one with a view to setting it off. For once I was glad when the younger gang members were told to clear off. We watched from a distance as my brother, Brian Reeves, Johnny Bullus and Johnny Walsh waited for the big bang. When this did not happen they all stuck their heads over the firework and guess what: it went off. The result was our poor old Mom rushing off to the doctors (again) with four screaming kids in tow, eyebrow less and hairless, returning covered in this bright yellow cream called Acroflavin. They thankfully survived the ordeal with no permanent injuries.

Our seaside holidays...

For two weeks in the summer, most of the industries in Birmingham shut down, called the 'industrial fortnight'. Special excursion trains were laid on to take all the working families on holiday. We always went to a bed and breakfast in Rhyl in North Wales. What a treat that was! All four of us would enjoy walks along the prom. One year, to my disgust – I cried about this – we hired bikes, but I was only allowed to have a three-wheeler, whilst his lordship had a two-wheeler.

Chapter Two

Enjoying our seaside holiday along the front at Rhyl: Mom, Dad, Aunt Anne, Uncle Len, Me, Our Kid and Cousin Dorothy.

The outside lavatory, and the maggots escape...

The only lavatory paper we ever knew was made from newspaper, specifically the *Daily Mirror*, the pages of which were torn up into four pieces and impaled on a nail on the inside wall.

Me and Our Kid were the same as any other boys swapping and collecting things. The classic was when Our Kid swapped for a tin of maggots, probably to go fishing. Not wanting to take these into the house he shoved them in their tin on the shelf in the outside lavatory and promptly forgot about them.

Enter Dad to do what comes naturally. Now Dad, working on the railway, drove in unheated cabs and therefore for warmth wore one-piece combination underwear which incorporated a back flap. The day the inevitable happened, I was playing in the yard and the chain of events went something like this. Dad sitting on toilet with trousers round his ankles, rear flap open. Dad hears buzzing noise. Dad locates buzzing noise to tin left by my brother. Dad opens tin. Tormented howl comes from inside the toilet. Door bursts open. Dad flies out of toilet, trousers round ankles, rear flap open, with hundreds of bluebottles in hot pursuit! Result: all dive for cover until Dad calms down and finds true culprit.

The garden and horse muck...

The houses in Wellesley Street all had their own back yards, with a coalhouse, a lavatory and what Dad lovingly termed the Back Garden. This consisted of two strips of land, one narrow and one super narrow, but Dad managed to grow chrysanthemums and snap dragons so Mom could have some flowers indoors. He once tried to grow a peony, but it never did flower.

On the narrow strip to the right of the yard was also the rhubarb patch and me and Our Kid were given the responsibility of collecting the horse muck from the milkman's and the baker's horses to feed it. This sounds easy on paper but in real life one had to contend with all the other kids in the street who had been given the same brief.

When Dad had his horse and cart we practically had our own supply with Dad keeping his eye out on his rounds to see if his steed would oblige. Dad used to pop in for a cup of tea when he was working close by, if he did it was our job to keep our eye on Trigger to see if he'd oblige whilst parked up. Our Kid used to stand on the wagon to prevent any usurpers who thought they had a chance at the coveted prize, while I held the nosebag so the horse could have his lunch and try to see if he would be helpful. We used to have wonderful rhubarb!

Chapter Two

Marbles and cigarette cards...

One of our favourite games was marbles. I remember Our Kid amassing a few hundred by winning them from the other kids, including playing for them in the gutter in the street. Mom never minded us doing this, even though those gutters were filthy, as she often said 'you need to eat a bucketful of dirt to keep you healthy' and it probably explains why our immune systems seem to have been in good nick ever since!

Another pastime was collecting discarded cigarette packets, found mainly in the gutter! In addition to the normal Woodbine and Park Drive packets, treasured rare additions were Passing Cloud, Three Castles, Sobranie Cocktails and Capstan Full Strength.

Dad smoked Woodbine Cigarettes. When he came home from work, he would smoke one or two, then have his supper and then enjoy one or two more before nodding off in his chair. From the age of about 13, Our Kid used to steal the biggest of Dad's nub ends and go out and secretly smoke them in the yard. That was until his 16th birthday, when Dad offered him a Woodbine out of his packet, saying that he was fed up with Our Kid nicking his nub ends! What a Dad, and what a plonker.

Chapter Three

Our grannies come to stay...

When I was about eight our grans came to live with us, Granny Johnson and Granny Cox, Mom's and Dad's mothers respectively. Granny Johnson was blind and nearly deaf, Granny Cox was deaf. Granny Johnson was as sweet as any Gran should be, but Granny Cox was something from the French Revolution. She would sit up the corner in widow's black and laced-up boots twiddling her thumbs wishing everybody would fall in the cut (canal), with the exception of me who she thought was lovely.

Having our grans was a major disruption. It eventually gave Mom bad health with the worry of them, especially knowing that Granny Cox was waiting to find fault and moan about it on a daily basis. On reflection she was an evil old woman. It also meant that me and my brother had to share a single bed in the small box room 'top and tailed' as it was called until our Grans passed away when I was 13.

On a lighter note, Granny Cox used to drink two pints of ale every night, and it was my job to go round to the outdoor at the pub with a jug to have it filled up. As this happened every night, I soon got into the habit of having a sup on the way back. This went on for some time but I must have got careless in my supping for one night Gran marked the jug and caught me out when I got back from the outdoor. I'm glad I only had two ear holes, I had a clip off Gran, and Mom, and Dad when he got home from work.

I did eventually get my own back. A law came out saying that kids could not carry open jugs of beer from the outdoor, so the breweries brought out a system where you had to take a bottle which was duly filled and a sticky label was wrapped over the stopper and the bottle. For a time I was stumped, until the barman left a pile of labels on the counter, light-fingered Malcolm soon saw the solution to his lack of a tipple. Those labels kept me going for some time and Gran's eyes were not good enough to see through the brown glass.

Chapter Three

Mom, Dad and their dentures...

Now, Mom and Dad were two totally different personalities. Mom was hustle and bustle and with a quick temper, Dad was laid back with a dry sense of humour, one of life's gentlemen.

Mom was four foot eleven inches, eleven and a half stone and built like a pocket battleship, but with a nice Mom shape. Dad was six foot four inches and eleven and a half stone – I've seen more fat on a greasy chip! They looked quite strange walking down the road, Dad's loping gait and Mom route-marching to keep up.

The combination of Mom's temper and her physique were quite formidable. Our Kid found this out early on in life and kept out of the way, but I was either fearless or stupid for I was always in trouble – looking back I think I was the latter. When me and Our Kid started fighting, Mom would chase us with the broom and I soon found out she was fully intent on using it: I was whacked many a time with the broom handle. Our Kid always seemed to escape, perhaps it's because he used to make sure he was first off with me trying to catch up hoping for protection: no chance!

I make Mom sound terrible but this is untrue, both me and my brother were little terrors and whilst our escapades were just the exuberance of youth we used to keep the neighbours on their toes and Mom ready to clip us one for misbehaving.

Dad could have been a professional glazier by trade. The gang used to play rounders in the street and me and Our Kid used to put windows through at regular intervals. Luckily for our neighbours there was a glazier shop up the street owned by a Mrs. Black. Dad must have had a credit account there for he was replacing windows every week in the holidays and you know I never heard him moan once. What a star.

Mom and Dad both had a complete set of false teeth; these were left in the kitchen on the windowsill every night steeping in Steradent. My favourite trick was to exchange Mom's uppers with Dad's. The following confusion and cussing was great but only if you kept clear of Mom's right hook, what a little horror!

His Royal Highness on bath night...

The houses in our street and in the area in general did not have bathrooms or hot water. We used to strip wash in the kitchen sink in the week and every Saturday was bath night. The copper boiler in the kitchen was filled with water and the gas lit, then the galvanised bath was dragged in from just outside the door in the back yard. We all took turns to have a bath, kids by two, then Mom, then Dad, all using the same water, lovely! Obviously you were on your honour to step out of the bath if you required a call of nature.

Now this worked fairly well until Our Kid reached his teens. At this stage in our lives me and my brother did not share the bath at the same time, but we still used the same water. Our Kid went first, of course, which turned out to be a bit of a problem. For some reason Our Kid had gone shy, bless him, perhaps embarrassed about his bits! The result of which was that he locked the kitchen door through to the sitting room so nobody could eat or drink whilst he soaked in his tub.

The more unfortunate side to this was that if you needed to go to the lavatory you had to go down the road, up the avenue, up the entry, down the yard and into the lavatory. What a plonker!

Another downside to Saturday night bathing once his Royal Highness had finished was to be in the bath while Mom cooked Dad's dinner. You see, me not being so shy, I had to contend with Mom carrying on with normal kitchen functions. Now our kitchen was not very big, so when the bath was brought in you could just get up the side of it to cook tea. This in itself was a nuisance more than a problem, but Mom always seemed to cook Dad sausages on a Saturday night and spitting hot fat hitting you from the sausages certainly made life interesting!

Then one night Mom was getting the sausages out of the pan when one got loose and dropped into my bath. Mom immediately went fishing for the sausage, when I said "What are you doing?" She said don't make a fuss as she had seen it all before! My Mom! She then retrieved and wiped the sausage, put it back on Dad's plate and threatened me with death if I blabbed. Well we were poor after all and Dad did enjoy his tea.

Flash Gordon and Hopalong Cassidy on Saturdays...

Saturday morning was ABC cinema minors picture show, it cost sixpence each and we had wonderful things to see like Flash Gordon, Lash Larue, Hopalong Cassidy and other great immortals from the silver screen. When it was your birthday you got a free invitation for you and a friend and you were on sentence of death if you didn't take your brother with you. This was not Mom trying to foster brotherly love, it just meant she saved a shilling!

Now we had an ABC minors' signature song, which I have no doubt my brother recalls, but knowing his track record for remembering things, here are the words:

Chapter Three

"We come along on Saturday morning greeting everybody with a smile
We come along on Saturday morning, knowing it's all worthwhile."

Christ this is boring, that's enough of that! As I have said before, Gordon Stanley always had money and on some Saturday mornings he would purchase stink bombs which we lobbed into the audience with gusto. Eventually the lights would go on, the film stopped and torches shone on to a bunch of angels who had not been fighting, kissing girls or doing any other naughty thing!

The risky side of going to the pictures was trying to act like the film heroes. I remember one Saturday we had watched Zorro, so when we came out of the cinema we promptly took off our Macs, buttoned them on like capes and charged through the gardens in George Street on our horses. We all had the sense to stop at the last garden at the junction with William Street except Stuart Reeves, who went over the wall and dropped about 10 feet. Oh well, another trip to the doctor.

Our football pitch...

At the top of Wellesley Street was a hall called the Mission, it was in fact an annexe of St. Silas School and was a meeting hall. There was a large area of ground behind the hall before the first house in the street. There were goal posts painted on the back of the hall and on the wall of the first house. The 'pitch' was covered in cinders with no markings, which made the game of football interesting and we played whenever we could find somebody who had a football. We tried to avoid playing with Gordon's ball because he used to go home taking it with him when his side was losing. We tried to tell him he could come back from being 56 to 0 down but he would not listen. The ground was used by the gangs around the area, but there was usually no friction when it came to playing there, unless it was the Harpers from Villa Street. Remember the hand-me-downs: well, the Harpers were not only poorer they smelled as well! Barry Harper even had my hand-me-downs!

I think back to playing on that ground and have to assume that the people in the first house were either very tolerant with the ball continually hitting that wall or they were just plain deaf.

By the way, for anybody who may read this masterful piece of literature, you may see the word Broc mentioned. This was Dad's nickname for my brother, me being called Nip. It is apparently derived from the term Brockton which is a Cockney corruption of the German word for brother. We still use it now: David is Broc I, I am Broc II and David's lad Mike is Broc III. Well there you go – back to the plot.

Chapter Four

Sunday afternoon tea...

My Mom's brother Len was married to Annie Raven. The Ravens were quite well off, they manufactured fireplaces and had a showroom in Brierley Street off Summer Lane in Newtown, Birmingham, and our Uncle Len was the foreman. Being comfortable money-wise, they could afford their own semi-detached house in a posher area of Birmingham called Perry Barr. They lived at 50 Tysoe Road off the Kingstanding Road and we used to go there every Sunday afternoon for Sunday tea. As kids we were very impressed because they had a proper garden with grass. This was only to look at, as Uncle Len would never let us play real football on his lawn.

Now you would think we were in Utopia when it came to presents from rich relatives. This turned out to be wishful thinking as far as me and Our Kid were concerned. We had two vests and two pairs of underpants apiece each Christmas and were told that when you reached fifteen you did not get any more presents because you were old enough to go out to work. I'm still trying to work that one out. I feel sorry for Our Kid though, he never got a proper job until he left university.

Underpants and a mortal dad...

Talking about underpants, as children until we were about eleven we all wore shorts. God Bless the invention of 'Y' fronts which appeared miraculously one Christmas. Before these appeared on the scene the underpants were like shorts and there was nothing worse than the leg of your underpants showing below your short trousers. How could you chat up your mate's sister with your knickers showing?

When you're kids you don't worry about things that do not affect your daily routines, but one day I saw Dad walking down the street bent over like an old man. I shouted for Mom who immediately ran out to see why I was shouting and then she saw Dad. She went into her formidable nurse mode and sent me for the doctor. We waited, sitting on the doorstep, anxiously wanting to know what had happened to the big lovable figure our Dad was to us. Eventually the doctor left and Mom called us in to tell us that a load had fallen off his wagon and hit him in the chest, the result of which was three broken ribs. Mom said we were not to worry, the doctor had said that he required complete rest for a week or so then he should be alright, which of course he was.

It made us realise that our Dad could be as frail as us mere mortals. Mind you: what a hero he was, better than any other Dad: he had broken three ribs, caught the bus home, said 'Hello Tich' to Mom and gone to bed. He was better than John Wayne!

Teenage arrogance...

As you grow up you start to feel you think you can rule the roost: as an arrogant teenager of fifteen I decided that it was perfectly alright to swear at my Mom. I remember the scene as if it was yesterday.

Mom and I used to argue at times and this one Saturday night we were having a right old go, all of a sudden I swore at Mom. I regretted it as soon as the words were out but I was too arrogant to say sorry. My brother, who then was eighteen, was sitting on the settee and Dad was in his armchair by the fire reading his paper. He slowly put his paper down and said "Apologise to your mother and, more importantly, to my wife."

Now being the thick teenage idiot that I was, I did not appreciate the second part of the statement, so I foolishly said "make me". Dad moved like a greyhound across that sitting room, I certainly did not see the bunch of fives coming and I definitely do not remember hitting the floor. I do remember coming round with my Dad applying a cold towel to my face with tears in his eyes. I realised immediately the pain I had caused my Dad in him having to strike me, I broke down and said I was sorry to Mom and it was all over. As I got up David made some comment and I shall always remember what my Dad said: "Don't think you are too old either, that's the first and last time I want to have to strike one of my sons."

My Dad was the gentlest of men and loved his sons. To this day I regret my actions that caused him so much pain.

Our cats, Mick and Tim...

We had a total of two cats, first Mick then Tim. Now Mick arrived the same time as me, so we grew up together. He used to wait for me in the street and when he

Mom and Tim.

caught sight of me, he'd come and walk me home. At Christmas we could not afford a turkey, so we used to have a capon which is a large chicken. Now this one Christmas, Dad had finished plucking the capon when Mick appeared down the yard dragging a chicken leg complete with feathers, none of your frozen rubbish! Mom took one look at Mick with this leg, which was nearly as big as him, sitting proudly at Dad's feet and said "Alf what are you going to do with that leg?" Dad answered in his usual dry humorous fashion. "Well seeing he's gone to so much trouble Tich, I had better pluck it for him." Mick sat watching Dad pluck his stolen gains and kept his eye on that leg until it went in the oven on Christmas Day and then sat in front of the oven waiting for it to cook, for his chicken was in with our capon. What a cat!

When I was fourteen I was out back when Mick came staggering down the yard. I shouted for Mom who ran out and gently picked him up, taking him indoors, waiting for Dad to come home from work. Dad got David to take me to Grove Lane baths to get me out of the house. When I came back, Mick had gone. Mom explained that Mick was an old cat at fourteen and had to be put down, for he had had a stroke.

Dad, bless him, tried to lighten what was an emotional moment for all of us by saying that he had also had a stroke, a stroke of bad luck, it had cost him ten shillings to have Mick put down!

Dad had buried Mick in the back garden but he would not tell me where in case I wanted a proper burial. I think he stuck Mick under his peony – for every year after that the peony was fabulous.

Mom soon sorted out my melancholy with a new cat called Tim, who was another character as Mick had been, mind you he had to swim at a very early age.

Tim's bath and an illegal party...

Mom, Dad and me went to Aunt Anne's one Sunday. Our Kid made the excuse that he had homework to do so stayed in. When we had had tea at Aunt Anne's, I was allowed home early to watch our new telly which had ITV. When I got home my brother had a full-scale party going on with his mates from Grammar School and their girlfriends and would not let me have the telly on. Enter one Della Horton, Our Kid's girlfriend, who said she had just put Tim in a bowl of water to see if he could swim. I ran into the kitchen and pulled Tim out of the bowl and dried him off. I went straight off her. I said I would tell our Mom about this party and his bird. He said I could have the telly on so long as I kept quiet. Oh! So easily bought!

Come Tuesday of that week I came home from school having forgotten the incident. I was met by Mom asking if there was anything going on when I had come back early from Aunt Anne's? I replied "No", having being sworn to secrecy. What I did not know was that Mom had found a grease mark on the wallpaper in the front room, which made her suspicious. She had also gone to the corner shop over the road which was owned by another Mrs Cox to buy some groceries, and she said to Mom: "Ada, I thought you said you didn't want any bread on Sunday, then your David came over for three loaves." What an idiot!

David came home from school and was confronted by Mom. He owned up to the party, apparently the grease mark was a Brylcreem mark off his mate Spick Spicer's head when he had been snogging with his girlfriend! Our Kid got told off for being deceitful but with no corporal punishment, even though he had used the front room. And me? I got preached at for telling lies, a good whacking to boot, and my cat nearly got drowned into the bargain, talk about favourites, thanks Broc!

The King George V...

Now our Dad working on the railway made me interested in trains, steam versions that is. Well, on one Sunday morning Dad said "Nip, the King George V has just been cleaned and is coming out of the sheds at Tyseley Depot, do you want to go and have a look?" There like a shot!

Now, being Sunday, I went out in my little grey double-breasted suit, shorts of course, with matching cap, talk about *Just William*. When we got to the station the

The King George V (courtesy Hugh Llewelyn).

train was there with steam up, me and my Dad were studying the engine when a shout came from the cab "Carlo (my Dad's nickname on the railway) do you want to bring the lad up onto the footplate?" I was up like a shot, I sat on the engine driver's lap looking at the instruments etc. when the magic words "do you fancy a trip up the line to the next station?" were uttered "and can your lad pull the whistle as we pull out?"

We were off, magic! We arrived at Leamington Spa and there we got off, Dad then cadged a lift back on a shunter and this is where it went wrong. The shunter was the workhorse of the yards and was obviously a bit dirtier than the George V, so when we got back into Birmingham my light grey suit was covered in smuts. My poor old Dad tried to wipe them off, but only made matters worse.

Now we both knew what Mom would say when we got home for Sunday lunch and I could see Dad was dead worried, so when we arrived I tried to say I had got too near the engine when it blew steam. She was not fooled, Dad got told he should have known better and I got a clip round the ear hole. Mind you, it was worth it, what a morning and I still enjoyed my Sunday lunch. Missed that skin again though, darn it.

Drunken Dad and no kiss tonight...

Once a year the lorry drivers at Dad's yard used to have a day out. It was always a Saturday and they organised a coach and went to the seaside or somewhere. Now Dad, bless him, could not afford to drink normally but he had saved over the year for the trip, so upon his return he was a bit merry and slightly unsteady on his feet. He was lovely; he enthused with love for me and Our Kid as any good Dad would. When it was time for bed, me and Our Kid would lie there giggling as we could hear Dad saying "Give us a kiss Tich", our Mom replying "get off, you stink of beer and you're drunk". This was followed by a swift kick in the ribs. I often wonder how me and Our Kid were conceived. Poor old Dad.

Chapter Five

Paper rounds and Gyp the dog...

I have already mentioned the formidable Mrs. Lewis who had the corner paper shop across the road on the corner of Wellesley Street and Guthrie Street. She never seemed happy and always had a scowl on her face, but I found out in my teens she had a heart of gold and whilst being abrupt she was a nice lady.

The reason I say this is that she asked Mom if I would do the paper round in our area. Now not only did it pay fifteen shillings a week, but more importantly she wanted to trust me, for it also involved fetching her cigarettes from a wholesaler named Frank Gibson in Wheeler Street, which meant I had to take a large amount of money with me when I took the order round. I also ran errands for her, so I took the job seriously.

Somebody apart from Mom and Dad trusted me and it was my first step on the road to taking responsibility, in other words growing up.

Mom made me give her my earnings, she gave me five shillings back and unbeknown to me put the rest into an account she opened for me at the Municipal Bank at Hockley Brook. My own bank book!

I thought it was great going round at seven o'clock in the morning whistling my head off (much to the annoyance of the neighbours) with the gang dog Gyp at my side. Gyp, a Staffordshire bull terrier, was actually Johnnie Walsh's dog, but he was my pal and we went everywhere together on that paper round. Mrs. Walsh would let him out every morning and I would find him sitting on our step waiting for me to start the round, he was great. Mind you, Mrs. Lewis would never let him in the shop, but she always had a bone or a treat for him when he'd finished his round. One of his favourites was a mint flavoured penny lollipop from Mrs. Cox's shop on the opposite corner. Thinking about it, he'd got the whole thing cracked.

In the winter Mrs. Lewis would make sure that I had a warm drink of cocoa or Bovril when I had finished the round before I went to school and when there was

Chapter Five

smog she'd supply me with throat sweets and cough mixture. Like other people in our street she cared for people around her.

Naughty words and messing with his girlfriend...

Now Our Kid being a bit older than me used to pick up the occasional naughty word and then used to tell me. I would not fully understand but it was obvious it went into the grey matter. These little titbits proved our downfall when we were invited to a party at Carla Millerchip's up the street. We were having a good time but this one little girl kept playing me up, and thinking of something horrible to say to make her go away, I thought of the latest grown-up titbit my brother had told me. I shouted "If you don't leave me alone I'll cut your cock off!" Result – both of us sent home from the party in disgrace, me getting the usual clip around the ear hole and locked in the back bedroom. My brother!

As you start to get a bit older you begin to look at those things you hadn't used to like: girls. Now Carol Reeves, Brian's younger sister, was a bit forward for her age and said to me one day "Do you want to play doctors and nurses?" I had no idea what she meant so she took me up the yard and let me look down her knickers. She said let me look at yours then: now this is where it gets a bit complicated. My Mom, that morning, had sent me out in shorts, shirt and jumper with braces under the jumper. In showing Carol mine I had to take my jumper and braces off and when she had had a look at mine I put my jumper back on first then my braces and went home for my tea.

When I got into the kitchen I got a right whack off Mom as I walked through the door. "What have you been up to you little devil?" she shouted. Quick as a flash I said I had been to the lavatory up the yard. "That's funny your Gran's in there so it must have been nice and cosy for the pair of you and what are your braces doing over your jumper?" I went straight to jail mystified, thinking Mom had eyes in the back of her head. What I had not realised was that Carol Reeves was Our Kid's girlfriend and he had heard me and Carol and run home to tell Mom. What a bummer! I still remember that first furtive look but for the wrong reasons! Mom told Dad to sort me out when he came from work. Dad, in his usual quiet manner, sat me down and said something about never playing too close to home, whatever that meant.

Coronation Year and his cardboard television...

The year of 1953 was Coronation Year, when Queen Elizabeth came to the throne. The Coronation itself took place in June. It was a really exciting time in

Great Britain, after the austerity caused by the Second World War. There were street parties organised, bunting put up and the streets marked out for races for all age groups. Everybody had a great time on the day. In our street we had races and events throughout the day with people dressing up. I remember Uncle Alf Bullus (they were all called Aunts or Uncles in the street) from across the road dressed up in a black frock coat and striped trousers down to his knees with white pumps on – we didn't know where he got it all from but he looked great!

Towards the end of the afternoon we went to Burbury Street School first for a fancy dress competition and then for a party. Now most kids went to the fancy dress in something with a Coronation theme: I went as John Bull, Roy Wilkins went as a horse guard. What did Our Kid go as? A television! He got a large brown cardboard box that Kellogg's Cornflakes packets came in, from across the road from Thomas's corner shop (it used to be that of the other Mrs. Cox but she'd left), and carefully cut the shape of a screen out. Dad painted some knobs on and told him he hadn't got a prayer of winning anything. He promptly stuck it over his head and entered the fancy dress competition for his age group and won it! He must have bribed the judges, though I don't know how because they couldn't see his angelic little face inside his box. There was a plus side to this mode of dress as well, for all he had to do once the competition was over was to throw his box into the playground and then proceed to create his usual havoc. The rest of us had to go and get changed for the party. A born leader of men!

Monday washdays...

Monday was always wash day up our street. The boiler would go on first thing in the morning, the mangle set up in the yard with the dolly, tub, scrubbing board and a thing called a Reckett's Blue bag which was put into the tub. I used to help Mom sometimes to do the washing because it was pretty hard work and labour intensive.

Mom would have to boil the sheets in the copper (i.e. the boiler) then bring them out into the yard in the tub and use the dolly.

The dolly comprised a long wooden shaft with a handle one end and a circular piece of wood at the other to which were attached four short pieces of wood. The modus operandi was to push the dolly into the clothes at the same time as twisting the four short legs in a clockwise and then anticlockwise motion which pummelled the clothes, forcing the blue through them, the effect being to further clean the washing, the blue making the clothes whiter.

Heavily soiled clothes were dragged out of the tub onto the scrubbing board for a good bashing. Once the correct standard set down by Mom had been

Chapter Five

reached, which was awesome, the clothes were then passed through the wringer which squeezed water out of the garments, which were then hung out on the line or if it was raining around the house. The whole process was terribly hard work for Mom (and all the other moms) and the smell of steaming clothes will always bring back the picture of Mom slaving away every Monday.

Chapter Six

Off he went to grammar school...

Our Kid was the first one to pass for grammar school in our street, everybody thought this was wonderful, but I eventually found it had its drawbacks. Dad did not earn good money on the railway so it was a bit of a struggle to find the money for my brother's school uniforms, books etc. This resulted in me having his hand-me-downs. To go to school in a barathea blazer with rolled collars and a dark patch where the Handsworth Grammar School badge had once been did not sit well on an up-and-coming gigolo. Mind you, most of your mates at school were in the same boat so nobody took the Mick.

One bright spot in the hand-me-down situation was that when I was fourteen I grew taller than my brother, me following our Dad. Our Kid followed our Mom, resulting in me having my own trousers. Great!

Not a perfect pupil...

He kept me up-to-date on what he was up to at his new school, including when he got 'six of the best' (not that he told Mom and Dad). He and another lad called Watkins were caught throwing snowballs from the playground into a classroom. They were marched along to the Headmaster's study, told to drop their trousers and the cane was administered across their buttocks. (Those were the days!) Our Kid nearly cried with the pain. However, Watkins was immune to the punishment, and despite the Headmaster giving him two more, Watkins continued to giggle throughout.

On another occasion, Watkins was bullying a weedy lad called Harrison and pushed him into a cupboard just as the master was entering the classroom to start a history lesson. After about five minutes, Harrison decided to leave the cupboard and walked over to his desk, passing in front of the teacher who was so amazed he was speechless. Harrison just sat down and the lesson continued without comment!

Chapter Six

Each week, the French teacher 'Baggy' Lindon would collect the dinner money from everyone – 2 shillings and 9 pence each – for the forthcoming five days. One particular week, there was not enough change to collect from all the class, so Baggy dictated that the next week everyone should bring the correct amount without change needed. Of course the whole class proceeded to bring the correct amount as pennies and halfpennies! Baggy was not a happy man – his desk was groaning under the weight of all that copper and imposed detention on everyone. He was also not happy in another lesson when in turn everyone had to speak a few words of French from a textbook and translate what had been said. A boy called Bob Brown had a sentence beginning 'Mon chien fidele' which he translated as 'My dog Fido'! (Instead of course 'My faithful dog').

David joined the school army Cadets, which meant he wore his soldier's uniform twice a week, on Mondays and Fridays. Being such a sensitive person, he couldn't tolerate the itchy khaki shirts that were provided, so Mom had to buy him a smart new expensive cotton one. He once went off with the Cadets for a week to the army's training facility at Castle Martin in South Wales and nearly got himself killed when he and his mate decided to have an illicit cigarette in a deep furrow in the middle of one of the practice fields and unexpectedly a tank came racing towards them. They jumped around a bit to warn the crew of their presence – successfully! – and were nearly court marshalled!

Our Mom was previously married to a guy who served in the army, some of that time being in Africa. He was killed in a motor bike accident. His 'legacy' was a display cabinet full of exotic butterflies, very beautiful. Mom agreed to give it to Handsworth Grammar School, and it was proudly hung in the biology classroom where we assume it still hangs.

The rat dissection...

He studied biology and in the sixth form was into the dissection of rats, so Dad thought he would help Our Kid's education by bringing a dead rat home from work for him to dissect. I thought this could be interesting so I duly helped by carrying the surgeon's instrument roll into the operating theatre: the shed.

He carefully washed the rat down with formaldehyde and then proceeded to make an incision in the corpse, explaining to his assistant the procedure and technique he was going to use. This was all very well until he cut into the stomach. The stink was awful! Nobody had told Our Kid that the rats used in dissection at school were specially bred for the purpose, having a controlled diet, unlike its cousin the sewer rat which ate anything. We could have died from bubonic plague that day!

During his years at the school, Our Kid had been swimming vice-captain, house vice-captain and athletics vice-captain – pretty impressive, really. However, one day his biology teacher Mr. Howdle told him 'Cox, you'll never be a Number One'. This really hurt our 'leader of men' and it was to prove a real motivator, as we shall see later.

Nitrogen tri-iodide...

He also studied chemistry in the sixth form, and I've checked this story of his by looking up nitrogen tri-iodide in Wikipedia, which states that this compound 'is an extremely sensitive contact explosive: small quantities explode with a loud, sharp snap when even touched lightly'. What he did, in the chemistry laboratory, was to add iodine to ammonia solution, pour the mixture, with its newly formed granules of nitrogen tri-iodide suspended in it, through a filter paper housed in a glass funnel, and left it to dry overnight. The next morning, just before his next chemistry lesson, he inquisitively – yes – lightly touched the dried compound. It exploded and obviously threw a cloud of it onto him and his mates such that during the lesson there were little explosions heard on them. Luckily the master didn't twig what was causing such interruptions, and even more luckily David was not blinded.

His school reports...

Incredibly, he still has all his school reports from his first school, Anglesey Street Primary, from the age of 7. Opposite is a sample, when he was 9 years old.

Equally incredibly, he still has every one of his grammar school reports which were provided at the end of each of the three terms per year. Here is a flavour – good and not so good – of some of the teachers' comments written on them:

"His work is interesting but he lacks patience." *(Art)*

"A cheerful boy who has tackled his work here with great enthusiasm." *(Biology)*

"He is weak in the imaginative side of the subject, strong in the factual." *(English)*

"I can't help feeling that he is not working to capacity in all his subjects." *(Year 3 end)*

"Weak. He is still below standard and hard work is necessary." *(French)*

Chapter Six

```
                Please retain for reference -
          CITY OF BIRMINGHAM EDUCATION COMMITTEE.
              ANGLESEY STREET PRIMARY SCHOOL.
   REPORT FORM FOR HALF YEAR ENDING 20th July, 1950
   NAME David Cox            CLASS   3
```

SUBJECT.	MARKS OBTAINED.	MAXIMUM.
ARITHMETIC:		
Written	19	20.
Mental	19	20.
Tables	20	20.
ENGLISH:		
Reading	10	10.
Composition	28	30.
Language	30	50.
Spelling	19	20.
Writing	18	20.
GENERAL KNOWLEDGE:	26	30.
TOTAL:	189	200.

REMARKS: David's work has balance and quality. He is a natural leader and a very intelligent child.

_____ Class Teacher.
_____ Head Teacher.
_____ Parent's Signature.

"He must discipline himself to several hours serious study every evening if he is to achieve real success." *(1st year 6th form end)*

And for an essay in the 6th form:

"The actual subject was ingeniously evaded. The argument was unstable theologically."

Chapter Seven

I start courting...

When I was sixteen I started courting my future wife Carole, she being fifteen: childhood sweethearts. I asked our Mom if I could bring Carole home for Sunday tea, Mom was delighted and told Dad to put on a collar and tie (Dad wore detached collars as was standard in those days). When we turned up for tea there was an argument about who was going to butter the bread and the wrapped sliced loaf was being thrown around the room between the rest of the Cox clan. As Carole walked in Dad said "catch it wench", which Carole duly did. Mom was mortified, one for being caught playing about on my girlfriend's first visit and two for Dad calling her wench.

Dad always called Carole wench much to Mom's continuing annoyance. Mom thought Carole was a little lady, which she is, and Dad thought she was too good for me, both thought the world of Carole. Our Kid could not see what she saw in me!

I happily went through my early teens, courting Carole.

I start my working life...

Having failed my eleven plus exam of which Mom kept reminding me bless her! I went to Gower Street Secondary Modern and left at fifteen. A lady up the road called Iris Millerchip told Dad there was an indentured apprenticeship in toolmaking at her company, Dennison Watch Case Company Limited. However: I had this grandiose scheme of doing graphic art but the mention of a proper trade to our Dad soon scuppered that, so a toolmaker's apprentice was what I became.

I was sent for the interview and it felt like conscription! I went to see Mr. Teddy Albaster, a lovely man, he was Works Manager. I must have shown promise as he called in the Foreman of the Toolroom, Mr. Alf Russell (another Alf!) who, again, interviewed me. I had done metalwork at school so was not totally dumb. I

Chapter Seven

was shown into the Toolroom which at the time had six Toolmakers and also the sections the Toolroom serviced. All lovely people, men and women. I was offered the job and accepted with the grand total of £1.10s.0d a week wage. My Dad had to come and see Mr. Albaster and Mr. Russell to confirm my five year 'conscription', sorry Apprenticeship! He had to give a character reference for me and he said I was a hard worker, honest, respectful and was keen to have the Apprenticeship offered. They thanked my Dad for coming so I took my Dad to the front of the factory, we were both a bit emotional but he was glad I would have a professional standing as a Toolmaker and I was glad to know that he had done his best for his youngest.

I knew how lucky I was getting my Apprenticeship for having gone to Secondary Modern School I had no qualifications and companies like Joseph Lucas Ltd and ICI required GCEs to become an apprentice. My Foreman informed me that I would be going to Handsworth Technical College to get my City & Guilds in Mechanical Engineering. God, I was so excited! Real qualifications, just like Our Kid. It would be one day a week, Wednesday, with homework and projects for the next five years. I thought it was wonderful and my Dad was well chuffed.

I was the first apprentice the Toolroom ever had and Mr. Russell was my mentor. I was joined six months later by a lad called Dougie Harryman and another called Peter Roberts, being the senior I was looked on as the leader of the three and this had its disadvantages.

We all learned very quickly that apprentices were like midshipmen in Nelson's navy, in other words at the bottom of the ladder. I had to call Alf Mr. Russell until he told me I could call him Alf and this took six months. The same applied to the other two, Doug had the Chargehand Mr. Eades and Peter had Mr. Newman, Senior Toolmaker, as their mentors. As three fifteen year old lads we were into everything, with a watchful Mr. R. keeping his beady eye on us. Having a Plating Shop, the Company used sulphuric acid in the electric plating process and glass carboys of the stuff were kept in the yard, so our first rollicking was for playing football and using carboys full of acid as our goal posts! We were threatened with suspension of wages if we did not behave. Our second escapade was managing to set fire to a bosh of whale oil used for hardening tools, resulting in two fire engines attending. That day, we did lose a day's pay. Alf, however, was philosophical about three kids together but always making us aware of how dangerous manufacturing could be if you did not listen to your elders so we settled down into our apprenticeship routine.

College – day release...

We all went to college on different days, I doing my City & Guilds, Doug and Pete doing National Certificate.

I had Theory in the mornings and Workshop Practice in the afternoon. My major project towards my Intermediate C&G was on Presses and Press Mechanisms. This was, of course, both in the workshop and the dreaded homework. I was sitting at home one night stuck on this project and Dad said "Are you alright Nip?" I said I was struggling with it and he did not know how to help me. He suddenly said "Ask your Mom". I said what would she know about it and then came the astonishing reply that, just before the War, she had been a Forewoman over a Press Shop of over 20 people. So I did as Dad said and asked my Mom and she was amazing. She would listen to me and help when I brought my work home. When we had finished the project, I submitted this to my Workshop teacher, Mr. Poole, for assessment and I got an amazing pass mark of 96%. Mr. Poole said my knowledge of the subject was incredible and I must have had a good Foreman to teach me. He could not believe it when I told him it was not my Foreman but my Mom! He then asked to meet her and discuss her history in manufacturing. I went home to tell her that Mr. Poole wanted to see her and she clipped my ear thinking I was in trouble but I told her why and took her the following week on my scooter to the college. I was amazed to see that 'Pooley' had tidied up his office and the workshop as if for the arrival of Royalty! The lads on the course wanted to know who was the lady in the blue duster coat and smart hat who was having tea and biscuits with Mr. Poole, I said that is my Mom and mentor. You can imagine their surprise. 'Pooley' was charm personified with her and told me I must be proud of her, blimey was I just. I took Mom home and to both of us it was a beautiful moment, both with a tear and proud of each other.

Old Friend...

Going back to when I was at Burbury Street Infants' School, I met what was to be my life-long friend, Dave Bishop (Bish). In fact, Bish finished up as an in-law as he married Carole's cousin Rosemary, who he met at our wedding and married 12 months later. Friends since we were five years old, Bish sadly recently passed away. Seventy years of friendship.

We shared many exploits during school and teenage years. We moved from Burbury Street Infants' School to Gower Street Secondary Modern. He was always a bit sharp and at the senior school he became 'Crisp Monitor', running the little tuck shop, and I was made a Prefect. I could never understand how he made a profit from selling crisps! This was obviously his natural bent and was the start of a career in Sales.

As a Prefect and the school being in a rough area, they were very interesting times. We, as Prefects, had to give out detention from time to time. This meant staying behind with the culprits so we gave them a choice – detention or a thumping, and surprisingly most of the time they opted for the thump as that meant we could all go home at the proper time!! One morning at Assembly, our Head Master stated that there would be an armistice on knuckle dusters and flick knives and the Prefects would be coming round to collect the weapons. Not a very popular move for either the Prefects or the Teddy Boys. Result, major scraps in the playground as we tried to confiscate said weapons.

When I was 13 years old, we had a Drama Teacher who formed us into groups in the main hall and said "Imagine you are a clock!" When he got to our group he said "Why aren't you working like a clock?" Bish said "The spring's bust!" Result – a row of eight of us bent over the desks and whacked with a No.10 black plimsoll.

A Wannabee Rock Group called 'The Panthers'...

Bish, myself and another mate called Terry King (Kingy) decided to form a rock band, Dave and Terry on guitars and me on drums, having played a snare drum in the Scouts. I went to Yardley's, a music shop at the bottom of Snow Hill in Birmingham and for the princely sum of £25.0s.0d., hard earned, I bought a set of Premier Royale drums – snare, small tom-tom, floor tom-tom and bass. I struggled home from Snow Hill to Wellesley Street with the drums draped around my person tied with string. When I crashed through the front door, remember this is a small terraced house we lived in, Dad said, "Bloody 'ell Nip, why couldn't you play the mouth organ like anybody else? You can't play those at home."

Dad being Dad said I had to learn to play them properly so he paid 7s.6d. for a twenty minute session at Yardley's. What a gent, he only earned ten guineas a week! This I did for two years, becoming competent on the skins. I took over paying for myself as quickly as possible to ease the pressure on Dad's wallet. Having the drums at home, I was itching to have a go so when Mom went shopping one Saturday morning I gave her 15 minutes and then started practising my paradiddles. All of a sudden, the door flew open and there was Mom. She said "You little beggar!!" and confiscated my sticks, taking them shopping with her. I did not get them back for two days. She must have had hearing like Goonhilly Downs.

Having these instruments and very little money, Bish, Kingy and I needed somewhere to practise our art. Kingy worked for his Dad who was a builder, and he had this brilliant idea. He said he could build his mom a coalhouse in the yard. We could then use the coal cellar, cleaned up, as our base. We took all the coal out, cleaned the cellar and Bish put in some electric plugs. It looked great! We met on our first night, excited, opened the cellar door and looked at twelve sacks of coal. Kingy, the plonker, had not got round to building the coalhouse. End of group. Bish and Kingy sold their guitars but I carried on with the drums, having a modicum of success round Birmingham but never quite making it to 'Six Five Special'. Eventually, I had to make a choice between college and qualifications or drums so, sadly, sold the drums.

When I was 50, my wife Carole asked me what I would like for my birthday and I said jokingly "A set of drums!" To my amazement she bought me a second-hand set of Premier Royale, a 12ft by 8ft shed and the sound proofing!! This was installed at the bottom of the garden, complete with electrics and sound system and I still play them to this day. My Missus – what a star!

Biking with Bish...

Like Our Kid, Bish and I used to go biking and decided to go around Norfolk via YHA hostels, making for Sheringham on the coast where Carole and her family were holidaying. We had a great time and upon reaching Sheringham, we encountered the steep hill going straight down into the town. Our bikes picked up quite a speed and Bish shot passed me shouting "I thought you said Norfolk was flat, Coxy!" We just managed to stop before the main cross roads at the top of the town.

Carole's Mom, Tilly, and her siblings were born and brought up in Sheringham. Once Bish and I settled in at our hostel, we went down to the beach, finding Carole with her family. All her uncles, aunts and cousins were there. This was the first time Bish met Carole's cousin Rosemary. We all had a great time and over the years have reminisced about the new teen craze of a coffee bar with a juke box and always remembered listening to Johnny Kidd and the Pirates singing 'Shaking All Over' – very daring at the time!

Bish, such memories – miss you.

Chapter Seven

Bish and Me in 2016.

Chapter Eight

Our scooters...

When I was 16/17, Our Kid upgraded his Vespa scooter giving me his old one – hand-me-downs again! He said he would teach me how to ride it so off we went to a quiet side road in Aston and having gone through the controls he sat on the back and said "OK Broc, let the clutch out slowly". So I twisted the clutch lever but did not depress it, resulting in front wheel up in the air, Our Kid falling off the back and me shooting off down the road, not knowing how to stop it so using my feet as brakes. I am sure smoke was coming off them!! I eventually depressed the lever neutralising the gears and by this time Our Kid had caught up with me and gave me a right rollicking. I had managed to stop only ten feet away from the main road.

    I really started to enjoy my old scooter so decided to update it a bit. The colour I chose, much to Dad's disgust, was salmon pink but it still needed some flashy bits so I purchased two big plastic eyes which I stuck on the front. Another thing in need of improvement was the horn cover so I thought I would sneak it into work on the Friday, polish it and craftily drop it into the chrome-plating vat with the plater (Charlie) not knowing anything. My plan was to fish it out very early on Monday morning. Monday came and I crept into the plating shop and there was Charlie holding my 18 carat plated horn cover in his hand!!! I had used the wrong vat. I had a clip round the ear and more than a good telling off. I was told to strip the gold off the cover and was dreading I would get the sack but Charlie, thank goodness, thought a glowing ear hole was enough. He, bless him, then polished the cover and chromed it for me. What a gent. It looked great on the scooter.

His bubble car...

Our Kid decided to upgrade from scooter to bubble car: an Isetta. I thought it was wonderful. It did not last long, however. He had started as a brewer at Ansell's Brewery (see Chapter Ten) in Birmingham so when the first Brewer's Dinner came round he had to wear an evening suit. I helped him get ready and even ironed his trousers. I told him not to drink too much (Ha!) as he insisted on driving his bubble car. About 3am I was shaken awake by Our Kid holding a crushed headlamp under his arm. He was certainly the worse for wear! He must have had tremendous faith in me as he wanted me to straighten out the flattened lamp at work the next day. I undressed him and put him to bed carefully and went out looking for the bubble car. What a mess.

Off he went to university…

Having survived to our later teens we obviously started going our separate ways. As I said earlier, Our Kid was the first in our road to pass for Grammar School, well he was also the first to go to university. Mom and Dad were really proud, sickening! David wanted to be a biochemist and he went to Birmingham University which meant he stayed at home. Why couldn't he have gone to Aberdeen or somewhere?

Amazingly, six pupils from Handsworth Grammar School all went to Uni together – David, Gerald (Gel) Weeks, 'Nod' Page, Bob Pearson, Ken Blackburn and Dave Bunn, so they would complete 10 years learning together, from 11 years old to 21.

Our Kid soon became embroiled in university life, starting with Saturday evenings at 'hops' at the Students Union. There he learned how to drink a yard of ale without spilling a drop, and to drink pints quickly in 'boat races', and learned many a 'rugby song' which to this day he'll happily sing for you, given the slightest encouragement. However, he never did learn all the words to the classic 'Ballad of Eskimo Nell' which one of his fellow students, Dave Powers, recited to a standing ovation each Saturday.

He also learned to play Contract Bridge which occupied many a Students' Union lunchtime and often some of the afternoons as well.

Obviously, the sacrifices made by Mom and Dad (and Me) to get him to this seat of learning were paying dividends.

But he did work very hard, attending lectures and carrying out experiments. One he remembers fondly was to test how well the human body stores vitamin C. This meant the whole class of 17 males and three females each swallowing a large vitamin C tablet first thing in the morning, then every hour or so finding out how much had been excreted in one's urine, using the laboratory beakers for collecting the liquid for testing. At lunchtime, all the beakers mysteriously disappeared, leaving only narrow-necked (one inch diameter) measuring cylinders for urine collection. The female contingent was not happy.

Yachting, waiting on table and harvesting grapes...

Having completed his first year, Our Kid and Gel and a dozen or so others decided to hire yachts for a week on the Norfolk Broads, even though none of them had sailing experience. They found there was a lot of mud in shallow waters and were lucky not to become totally stuck a few times. They found the Broads' pubs very conducive to student behaviour, but of course they were never fully out of control.

After that, David and Gel had arranged four weeks working as waiters in a hotel in Lytham St Anne's. They lasted two weeks: Gerald went down with a severe cold, the owner couldn't accept paying a casual labour student sick pay, kicked them both out, and so, determined not to go home early, off they both went to search for more employment in Blackpool (just up the road) which they found in a laundry. It normally only employed local ladies but were short of staff. Those ladies adopted our poor student duo and plied them with cakes and pies! They found the cheapest B & B they could, with a double bed that had a big dip in the middle, so every hour or so through the night they finished up in a heap in the centre of the bed and had to crawl back up to opposite edges.

After that (noting that the summer vacation was 12 weeks long), the two of them went grape picking for three weeks in France, at a Gevrey-Chambetin farm near Dijon where they were introduced to big chunks of bread and cheese plus wine every lunchtime, and a farmhouse toilet which was a deep hole dug in the ground with two bits of wood to stand on either side of this hole with half a shed built over it for part privacy. At the end of the harvest, they left with a bottle of brandy each and enough money to spend two nights only in Paris, arriving back home in Birmingham penniless and unshaven.

So, that first summer vacation was memorable from start to finish.

The Midland Jazz Club...

Now in his second year at Uni, another venue became a favourite on Saturday evenings: the Midland Jazz Club held in the Digbeth Civic Hall, Birmingham. Dave Bunn's father was a sergeant in the police (stationed in Aston) and on Saturday nights he was the doorman at the jazz club. Our Kid and his mates never did pay the entrance fee, and in return plied Dave's dad with pints.

More importantly: it was here that David met Peggy, who David married some years later.

Chapter Eight

Sub aqua in Ibiza...

His second year at Uni went as the first: very hard work, apparently, and he survived it, so we'll skip straight on to his next adventure during the next summer vacation.

David had always been a good swimmer, so joined the university sub aqua club, which had training sessions in the pool at the neighbouring King Edward VI School. The University Head of Physical Education Bill Tuxworth became a great friend, and David was invited to be part of a scientific expedition to Ibiza, funded partly by the Royal Navy. He was one of the crew chosen to sail the boat hired from the Isle of Man, laden with loads of sub aqua gear, and spent a month down in Ibiza which in the early 60s had hardly ever seen a tourist. No, it doesn't sound like hard work: the only scientific objective was to assess the effect of depth on brain activity which the Royal Navy had examined but only in their pressure tanks in Portsmouth. All Bill Tuxworth (who could descend to 100 feet and more with only his snorkel) had to arrange to satisfy the funding was for one of the guys to be strapped to a ladder with lots of aqua lungs for company, be lowered to 150 feet, and be presented by his colleagues with blackboards with sums written on them. David was one who swam down to present some of the sums, so he can claim to have dived to that depth (and had to be careful to decompress on his way back up to avoid 'the bends').

A Frenchman friend of Bill joined them for a few days, and was equally a superb sub aqua expert. He demonstrated how to kill an octopus with his bare hands: either bite it between the eyes, or turn it inside out. No, none of them ever did try either method.

Our Kid's graduation...

Dad was 52, David was 21 and had passed with honours as a Bachelor of Science. How proud we were as a family. Mom went around telling all the neighbours and I'm sure Dad went around telling all his workmates.

On 14th August 1962, it was the graduation ceremony at Birmingham University complete with caps and gowns. Mom had a new dress for the occasion and Dad got out his best suit. Unfortunately we were only allowed two tickets for the investiture so I could not go and see my brother get his cap and gown, but Mom and Dad came back full of the occasion and we were all very happy.

Graduation.

Chapter Eight

When our world stopped...

Just two days later, on Monday night, 16th August our world stopped. Dad had complained of chest pains on the Sunday and Monday and that night he had a major heart attack and died in David's arms. Our loss was enormous. Our stable world was torn apart with Mom obviously totally distraught.

We had the funeral and tried to get on with life but Mom was inconsolable and six weeks later when I came home from work for my lunch I found our Mom had committed suicide and was dead in the kitchen. We had gone from being two lads with a loving home to the depths of despair in a short period of time, me 18 and Our Kid 21.

We now only had each other and the bond we had before was even greater now. We had Uncles and Aunts but we survived together, our love and support for each other seeing us through. Because David was twenty-one he was allowed to have his name on the council rent book, so we were not put out of the house.

We had to come to terms with looking after ourselves, my brother was my guardian, as being under twenty-one I was classed as an orphan. He would not let me have anything on credit, just like Mom!

David wanted to get a job after Mom and Dad died but he had set his heart on being a brewer, which required another post-graduate year at university studying malting and brewing. I said that Mom, Dad and even me had not made all these sacrifices for him to not achieve his goal, so we bit the bullet and he stayed on.

When Mom and Dad died, Tilly and Les, Carole's mom and dad, soon became second parents to me. God, I loved them, and soon started calling them Mom and Dad. I knew my parents would not have minded. Both were lovely and supportive all my life and I count myself very blessed that I met them when I did. They eased my pain considerably.

My apprenticeship continues...

I was in the middle of my Apprenticeship when our parents died.

When I returned to work the Monday after Mom's funeral, Alf, my Foreman said "Alright Son?" and to my astonishment handed to me a wrapped bacon and egg sandwich that his sister Rose, who worked on one of the sections, had cooked for me. Alf was a serious man and did not show much emotion so I was more than a bit overwhelmed by his kindness. This routine carried on every morning until I was 20. In this period, once the pain of loss had subsided a bit, jokes at Alf's expense were made by the Toolmakers. One of them said "Blimey Alf. For a confirmed bachelor you are sure looking after your little chick!" I cannot repeat

Alf's reply but I realised that I loved him anyway. He did not need kids at home when he had three at work!

At this time, I moved from the Toolroom into the Drawing Office. My old sponsor, Iris, having told the Works Manager I was good at drawing.

Closer than ever...

The entire trauma had brought David and me closer together than I think normal siblings usually are.

We had to learn to cook, wash and iron. The rent on the house was two guineas a week. I earned four guineas a week and Our Kid had a university grant of £350 per year, so sometimes the money got tight and we used to scrounge meals, me off Carole's family and Our Kid off his girlfriend Peg's family and anyone else who would feed us. Our Kid once tried to kill us twice with his cooking! He prepared 'Creole sausages' (just sausages boiled with tinned sliced tomatoes!). God bless Mrs Beaton. "Is that it?" I said. "I've been on a lathe all day." Although feeling a bit unappreciated, he took it to heart and tried to poison us another way the next night.

I became engaged to Carole that Christmas and David to Peggy.

We obviously from then on started to go our different ways, David having a career in the brewing industry and myself in engineering.

Chapter Nine

The Millerchips...

Going back in time a little: I have mentioned Iris Millerchip before, as the lady who suggested my Apprenticeship. She was married to Ray and had a daughter called Carla, who was about 5 years younger than me. I was about 14 at the time when Iris asked Mom if I could sit with Carla when she came home from school. They lived only five doors up from us and I did not mind because they had a telly!

Friendship with Iris and Ray blossomed and they started taking me on holiday with them. Iris saw some potential in me at this early stage and got me interested in reading, buying me I-Spy books. I have still got the first book she bought me called 'The Opal Seekers', which I treasure. Iris and Ray moved from Wellesley Street to Hylda Road, Handsworth, and I used to cycle over there to see them. Carla had made friends with a little girl the same age, who lived at No. 5 in the same cul-de-sac, called Pamela. She had an older sister called Carole, who was 15 and we were introduced. It was love-at-first-sight for me at the age of sweet 16. We started going out together and got engaged, Carole at 18, me at 19, and were married at 20 and 21. Having told her it was love-at-first-sight for me, she tells me she had to work at it!

Politics...

Ray Millerchip was a Labour Party Birmingham City Councillor for the Newtown Ward, so when I went to look after Carla I started to help by folding leaflets for the Municipal elections and delivering them around Newtown. When I was old enough (16), I started canvassing for the Party at election times, with a group of other young people, including Carole. Ray was keen on setting up a Young Socialists' section so he asked me to help form it. I became Chairman of the Young Socialists for Newtown and Secretary of the Newtown Labour Party. I also became Election Agent, first for Ray, then Charles Horton and then Harold

Meredith, being successful each time. I think I am still one of the youngest Election Agents the country has had.

Changing jobs...

As already mentioned, in June 1965 Carole and I got married and rented an unfurnished flat in Handsworth. The rent was 5 Guineas a week, and sometimes this was a bit tight but we managed. I was still a Draughtsman at Dennison's and Carole was a Secretary at Lucas's in Great Hampton Street, Birmingham. When I was 22, Dennison's started to have financial problems and I was, unfortunately, made redundant. I remember it well, it was a Wednesday and Teddy Albaster called me into his office. He was nearly in tears. He said he wanted me out quickly as British Leyland were on the point of getting rid of 3,000 workers and he wanted to give me a chance of getting another job before all their engineers flooded the market. On the Thursday morning, I went to an employment agency, who sent me to a company called Metal Closures Ltd. in West Bromwich.

I went to see Derek Day, Personnel Manager at M.C.L., who thought I would make a good Draughtsman in their Development Department. Now, M.C.L. made what the public would call bottle tops but he said that the Development Manager would be more impressed if I called them 'closures'. I went upstairs to meet Mr. Ron Wilton, the Manager, who was small, dapper, with a quiet, calm manner, thank goodness. He said he wanted someone with Toolroom and Drawing Office experience and I seemed to fit the bill. The interview, would you believe, took two and a half hours. It was obvious that he had forgotten more engineering than I would ever learn. He asked me when I could start and I said the following Monday. I had got the job. A man called Ken Imlay took me down to the shop floor and, coming from an environment that made watch cases and was reasonably quiet, imagine my horror when I walked onto the shop floor and saw about 200 pieces of kit making bottle tops, sorry – closures. At each stage of manufacture plastic tubes were being used to blow aluminium shells from one machine to another. The noise was terrible. I said nothing as I was just relieved to get a job. I phoned Carole to tell her that I had got the job but didn't know if I could do it but it would be alright for now. I was there for 30 years! When I got back to Dennison's later that day I went to see Mr. Albaster to give him the good news. He was delighted. Next day on the Friday, I was saying my goodbyes and he called me into his office. He wished me well and presented me with a set of Swiss drawing instruments, very expensive and state-of-the-art. He said they would help me in my career. A really kind man. He and I were both upset as I had been there for seven years but things change and time moves on.

Chapter Nine

Metal Closures Ltd...

Metal Closures Ltd. supplied screw caps for glass and plastic bottles for the distillers, pharmaceutical and soft drinks industries around the world. M.C.L. was in Bromford Lane, West Bromwich, and the Development Drawing Office was next to the Chairman's office and the Board Room. Best behaviour at all times. I soon found the work interesting and fascinating as, apart from designing the closures and tools for making them, we also worked on other equipment around the factory. We had another factory nearby in Kelvin Way, which made machinery for putting the closures on bottles so I also designed for these. I started as a Junior Draughtsman, working my way up to Senior Draughtsman. At around this time, we moved from Bromford Lane to the Kelvin Way site, not only for developing new products but developing new machinery for producing and applying closures. All of this time I was attending night school to get senior qualifications as an engineer. Seven years of this, finishing when I was 28 years old. As a qualified engineer, joining the Institute of Production Engineers and the Institute of Packaging, Carole and Our Kid were very proud. At that time, my Company asked

Me as a Turk.

Chapter Nine

me to represent them on the Technical Sub-committee of the Metal Packaging Manufacturers' Association (M.P.M.A.). Ron Wilton was Chairman of our group on this Sub-committee and together with other companies we set the standards for the industry. Not only did we design the closures for our customers but also designed the glass finishes for the customers' glass bottles and other closure products for the canning and drinks industries. I also represented M.C.L. on a European Standards Committee (C.E.I.T.E.), who worked on International Standards to ensure best working practice for the industry.

On the careers front, I seemed to be doing well and on the social side a friend from Lichfield said if I needed to let off steam and get a bit of exercise then I should join him and some mates playing Squash. This I did, enjoyed it immensely in spite of several injuries and played with this gang until I was about 60.

When I was 35, M.C.L. along with an Australian company, decided to develop an ecology can end, where nothing, such as a ring pull, would come off when opened. I was made Chief Designer for this major project for M.C.L., forming a team to produce the tooling and ancillary equipment. About three years into this project when production was about to start, John Cassera, our Chairman, came over and told me we had done a deal with Allied Breweries to supply the can end to their Burton Brewery. You can imagine his amazement when I told him that the Managing Director of that brewery was none other than Our Kid (see Chapter Ten). He had not recognised or connected the Cox name. I thought it was incredible that the paths of David, a biochemist, and me, a mechanical and production engineer, should cross in this way in manufacturing. What about that Mom and Dad?!

The funny side to the Ind Coope/Metal Closures Group relationship, was Our Kid being invited to visit our factories and have lunch with the Chairman and Directors. I would not normally be involved in such an event but Our Kid insisted that I should have lunch with them all. Thanks Broc. It was a funny feeling sitting down to lunch with my brother in those circumstances but a great moment.

Unfortunately, recession hit the UK just after this. Companies tightened their belts and our can end production was dropped when customers went back to using ring-pulls because they were cheaper. The Company decided to diversify and formed a partnership with an American company, H.C. Industries, to make plastic closures for the drinks industry. The factory at Kelvin Way was converted into a full production unit, with a back-up Tool Room and Drawing Office. This was an exciting time as I was developing both aluminium and plastic closures with new technology (see Chapter Ten).

Changes...

By this time, Ron had long retired and a reorganisation was taking place under a new Chairman, who wanted to revitalise Development and Production areas. In 1990, I was promoted to Metal Closures Group Development Manager and also responsible through my team in assisting in the Production areas. This proved to be a fascinating and demanding job in both areas.

My role included technical liaison with customers, working with the Sales Department, headed up by the Sales Director, Don Harrold. We worked very well together and became firm friends. I started travelling the world for Metal Closures Group, who had factories in South Africa, West Indies and Italy, as well as licensees throughout the world. In America, Don and I shared stand duty in Chicago and we also did trips up the Napa Valley wine-growing area in California, trying to get customers interested in aluminium screw caps for wine, which M.C.L. had been developing to replace cork. Interesting times.

During these years ownership of the Company had changed a couple of times and in 1995 the new owners decided to 'reorganise'. They did not perceive that they required Development and Technical Departments so, at a stroke, myself, the Technical Manager, the Service Manager, the Chief Chemist and our teams were made redundant, all on the same day. Too many bricks out of the wall.

Changing Careers...

I started to receive requests for technical information from various contacts in the trade as they said there was no longer any technical back-up from my old Company. At this point, Carole suggested that there was clearly a need so I should set up as an independent Packaging Consultant. I took her advice and did exactly that, with immediate success. I started giving lectures to the Glass Industry and became their independent technical advisor and, low and behold, M.C.G. now under a different ownership wanted me back in to train personnel. This I did and was retained for two years. At the same time, a company called Irish Metal Closures, who had a technical agreement with M.C.G. for many years, found they had lost the technical back-up so James Fox, their Managing Director, approached me to work with them as their Technical Consultant. They wanted to increase production and improve their technical base, so I designed and introduced new production lines for them and carried out in-house training. I had known James and his father John, who was Chairman, for many years whilst working for M.C.G. and had developed a very good relationship with them and the Irish company.

Chapter Nine

Cussons International, the pharmaceuticals giant, also contacted me to help them with production requirements. They asked me to go to India on their behalf to look at production equipment for making cans to contain medicated talcum powder, for production in Nigeria. I spent a couple of weeks in India, finally recommending a company to supply the equipment, which they accepted and the line was purchased.

I worked as an independent Technical Consultant in the Packaging Industry for over ten years and retired at 65, feeling that my career of 50 years in manufacturing had been diverse, interesting and successful.

Chapter Ten

Postgraduate student in malting and brewing...

After our traumatic summer losing Mom and Dad, it was back to Birmingham University for a fourth year for Our Kid, this time in the School of Malting and Brewing, under the leadership of its new professor, James S Hough.

His first memory was to join the exclusive 'Firkin Club', only open to students of the School, the entrance requirement for which was to be able to drink a firkin of ale (that's 72 pints) in a week, which he found easy.

The second was to realise that the professor's family was no less than the renowned producers of sanitary ware, thus his middle name 'Shanks' which is emblazoned on all their produce as 'Armitage Shanks' (Armitage being a Staffordshire village). From that day to this, Our Kid has taken pleasure from the thought that whenever he uses one of their urinals, he is urinating on his professor.

The course went well, especially that part where he had to go and work for three weeks during the Easter vacation in a maltings, with Pauls Maltings in Ipswich accepting him for this. Its R & D director was Ollie Griffin, who became a lifelong friend, and instead of leaving David to continuing shovelling grain in the maltings, invited him to join him for his third and last week on a visit to the distilleries in the Spey Valley, Scotland. Each day's routine became: arrive at the distillery at 10am, go to the stills, sample the whisky being produced (with the essential offer of Scottish spring water to go with it), and ... he can't remember what happened for the rest of the day until arriving in some pub or other to start again and rest for the night.

He graduated with an M.Sc. in Malting and Brewing.

A brewer at Ansells Brewery...

David joined Ansells brewery for his first job in October 1963, for the then princely salary of £1,000 per year. He immediately became a favourite of the then

Chapter Ten

Head Brewer John Burton, who quickly introduced him to the habit of having a meeting with him at 10 every morning in the sample room.

An early memory was that there were numerous occasions when the brewery fire alarms went off, and there was great admiration for a young fireman (employed by the brewery) who was always quick to find where fires were starting

Me and David at one of his formal dinners.

and put them out. The brewery only found out later that he was starting them! A pyromaniac fireman!

Another important memory was that he married Peggy in 1966.

Brewing did not always go smoothly. One day a colleague brewer, Bill Cook, started 10 tons of malt mash into one of the mash tuns to start the brewing process but had forgotten that a side door in the tun (used to evacuate spent grains from the previous mash) had been left open, and most of the mash poured out over a director's car that had been parked in the yard underneath. Bill luckily survived!

With his Brummy accent, Our Kid got on well with the workforce as well as doing well with the technical side, so pretty soon he was trusted with having a master key which opened every brewery door. This included a wicket gate entrance to the brewery half way up the side street (Park Lane) away from the main security gate (which was manned 24 hours a day). One Saturday evening he invited me to join him for a pint or two in the brewery: we went unseen through the wicket gate and tried a few ales in the sample room before letting ourselves out the way we had gone in! What a treat!

It was not the only treat I enjoyed with him as a brewer at Ansells. Every year, he attended formal dinners at the Midland Hotel in Birmingham and invited me to be his guest at more than one of them. I used to smoke in those days, and after the meal and the Royal Toast, Cuban cigars were offered to everyone, and despite the fact that most of my fellow guests didn't smoke, they accepted theirs and gave them to me. They kept me going for weeks afterwards. Not only that, I knew that we were always into a heavy night drinking to the early hours so I always pinned a note inside my dinner jacket with my home address written on it, to show the taxi driver just in case I was completely incoherent!

Across the road from the brewery was the then famous HP sauce factory, which had its own brewers making vinegar for its sauces. Invited to their sample room, David tells me that it was amazing to be asked to identify the difference between the tastes of their six-month-old vinegar versus younger batches! When all we ever did was splash any vinegar offered on our chips!

When he was only 30 years old he showed once more that Our Kid was a leader of men: he was appointed Head Brewer. It was soon afterwards that he was summoned for Jury Service. On arriving at the Law Courts in Birmingham to fulfil this duty, the clerk took his details including that he was no less than the Ansells Head Brewer. The clerk was horror struck: "I drink Ansells bitter, who's going to look after that while you're in court?" he asked. When told it was a bit of a risk to his favourite tipple to have the Head Brewer away for what might be weeks, he duly excused Our Kid from doing his duty, so he never did serve.

Chapter Ten

David and Peggy.

This is nothing to do with the story! But here's a pic of the family dog Archie, a pedigree Fox Terrier, enjoying his favourite pint of Pedigree at The Fox, Shenstone.

However, there was a sting in the tail: the legal case he missed was against the then Cinephone Cinema in Bristol Street for showing naughty (mainly French) films, and the jury, without him, had to sit through days of seeing these films to form their judgement! So, still a plonker!

One important moment at around this time came when he was invited with Peggy to the wedding of the daughter of Mr Geoff Howdle, who, when he was biology master, had said to Our Kid all those years ago at school "Cox, you'll never be a Number One". David duly presented him with a business card saying 'Head Brewer'. It's funny what spurs you on in life – I'm sure Our Kid had been harbouring the thought of never being less than Number One all those years after being our leader back when we were in Hockley.

Chapter Ten

Just before embarking on the next stage of his career, several crates of strong old ale were found in a disused cellar at the brewery, and Our Kid managed to acquire one of them. For several years, Peggy's mother Dorothy made the best Christmas puddings you have ever tasted, apparently – he never gave me any.

And so to Burton...

Peggy and he had a daughter Jane, born in 1968 and a son Michael, born in 1970. They had first lived in Walmley, and then Erdington.

Ansells had become, along with Tetleys and Ind Coope, part of Allied Breweries. And so it was that in 1976 at the age of just 35 he was promoted to Head Brewer of the Ind Coope Burton Brewery (one of the top three biggest breweries in the UK).

At that time in the late '70s, CAMRA (the Campaign for Real Ale) was at its most robust, and Ind Coope with its Double Diamond keg beer (the antithesis of Real Ale) was a sworn enemy. It was time for Ind Coope to respond, which it did by asking Our Kid to present a proper Real Ale which he duly did, to his personal taste. It went to market as Draught Burton Ale. What a joy as Head Brewer to have invented such a brew! (Its sales peaked at 100,000 barrels per year, but sadly, as brewed at Burton, it is no more.)

As well as that memory, amongst many whilst at Burton, another is foremost. During that time he went to London Business School on its 12-week flagship course, the London Executive Programme. The Principal of School at that time was Jim Ball (later to become Sir James), an eminent world economist. Our Kid was chosen to be the President for the first week of the programme, to represent course delegates to the faculty for queries, issues arising and so on. But the major task of that first week was to preside, as Chairman, over the inaugural dinner, a very formal occasion with all faculty and delegates present, with him seated at the centre of the top table flanked by Mr. and Mrs. Jim Ball. Our Kid had to respond to an extremely erudite introduction speech given by Jim. He did so by stating that he had worked out the mystery of why he had been given the honour of being chosen to be president for this first week: it was because "I, David Cox, could tonight stand before you erect between two balls". He immediately then turned to his left to apologise to Mrs. Ball for his crudity, only to find she had collapsed on the floor with laughter! Despite having his formal notes ready for continuing by saying all the appropriate 'great to be here' remarks, he couldn't deliver them because the whole room was in unstoppable laughter, so he just sat down and said nothing more! That's Brummy upbringing for you!

And then to Warrington...

Our Kid had become unstoppable! Off he went in 1979, with Peggy and their two children Jane (then aged 10) and Mike (aged 8) for him to be in full charge (as Director) of another of Allied's breweries, Tetley Walker, in Warrington.

He even inherited his own chauffeur, Tom. This is his fondest memory of him: Our Kid's own company car was a 3.5 litre Rover. One day he drove home with a 10 litre tin of emulsion paint in the boot, and the next morning discovered that the lid had come off and the carpeted boot was fully painted. So he just drove it next morning to the brewery garage, parked it, told Tom 'there is a bit of a problem in the boot', and then calmly drove it off in the evening without a word being said. The boot was immaculate! There were plenty of laughs to go round over the following days.

His biggest 'perk' as a Director was that he was enrolled onto 'the kipper list'. A subsidiary of Tetley Walker was Ind Coope Isle of Man. To be on the 'kipper list' meant that a box of the best kippers in the world, Manx kippers, were posted every month to your home by that company.

My most vivid memory of him at Warrington was when there was a strike at the brewery – which lasted a phenomenal ten weeks. During that time I was watching the BBC 6 o'clock news when there was an item about the strike and there were the brewery pickets holding banners proclaiming "we are all out to get Foxy Coxy and Co."! It's the only time he'd been mentioned on national TV! Also, apparently (he tells me) there were 'flying pickets' driving round to all the Tetley Walker pubs during the strike, and he was having a pint in one of them (whilst they still had beer to sell) when a couple of these pickets happened to visit it: he offered to buy them a drink but they declined and disappeared fast! No sense of humour there!

And back to Burton...

He (and the Warrington brewery) survived the strike and in 1982 he was appointed back to Burton as Managing Director of the Ind Coope Burton Brewery. I can't imagine what Mom and Dad would have said about that!

He and his family settled back into the Midlands, living in Shenstone near Lichfield, which they did for the next 30 years.

He was invited in his first couple of weeks at the brewery by 'the Shop Stewards Committee' to join them for a drink in the Ind Coope Sports and Social Club, and he asked me to pick him up on the evening at the end of the event. He knew it would be a 'baptism of fire' when they would test his drinking capacity, so by the time I arrived he (and they) were well gone. I had to step in and protect my brother from their late onslaught – rather amusing to defend him in those circumstances – but he hardly needed my help, as, like always, he was able to look after himself. I'm sure that that day he gained their personal respect in his new role having survived in one piece.

One memorable day was when the brewery hosted the Lords Taverners, challenging them to a cricket match at the Sports and Social Club. John Arlott, the renowned cricket commentator, who had retired and lived on Alderney in the Channel Isles, was invited, so a chauffeur-driven car was sent down to pick him up, with the necessary few bottles of Beaujolais in the boot. David Frost was amongst the guests and arrived ostentatiously in his Rolls Royce. No one can remember who won.

Our Kid did appear on TV again: ITV did a series of programmes on Midland towns, one devoted to Burton upon Trent. They caught him on camera at one of the brewers' monthly PDPU's (Pay Day P— Ups) in a local pub, and he had to explain to the programme presenter what PDPU meant, which was noticeable on the 'club' tie he was wearing. It featured prominently on the subsequent programme. David thought he was due for the sack over that, but his boss thankfully thought it was highly amusing!

He was Managing Director until 1988, and the whole of those six years were devoted to what became a major redevelopment of the Brewery. It was successful, so we won't spend any time relating that story.

And then at 47 years old and 25 years to the day after he had become a young brewer at Ansells, Our Kid decided to leave the brewing industry, to start up on his own as a management consultant.

As management consultant...

Since his attendance on that Executive programme in 1978 at the London Business School, he had maintained contact with the faculty there and had been invited to give a few lectures during his successful project in the '80s at Burton. This started him acquiring clients who needed advice on managing change, and his new career took off. Over the next few years, he accumulated clients across the world, including California, Canada, New Zealand, Australia, Hong Kong and France, as well as many in the UK. He loved the freedom of being his own boss, and meeting and advising so many people in senior positions in their Companies, who actively wanted to develop themselves and their organisations.

His most satisfying relationship became one with Templeton College, part of Oxford University. Anderson Consultants teamed up with its faculty to run a series of one-week programmes for their new recruits, and David was chosen to present his brewery experience as a 'case study' as part of it. It was a roaring success, so much so that Anderson sent a couple of senior directors from the USA to see why the results were so much better than they were achieving on their homeland courses. Result: the programme was exported and repeated several times in the US, at Emory University, Atlanta, including Our Kid.

David's son Mike was a beneficiary of his Dad's consultancy activities. Firstly, after David had done a lecture tour of Australian cities (Adelaide, Sydney, Melbourne, Canberra, Brisbane) and met and worked with several chief executives, many of them invited Mike, now 18 years old, to stay with them, so a tour was organised for him which lasted for no less than eight weeks. Our Kid joined him for the last two weeks of that in Melbourne and they spent a few days touring together, then went to Barwon Heads Golf Club, Melbourne, where David was running a three-day workshop for a fertiliser company. The guys on the course effectively adopted Mike, who spent the full three days playing on their magnificent course. (Mike was by then a good golfer with a handicap of 10).

Next treat for Mike: David had a client (Hong Kong Telecom) in Hong Kong, and at the time Virgin Atlantic was introducing flights there and offered an introductory 'two flights for the price of one'. As a result, the two travelled business class at the client's expense for a week in Hong Kong, no charge for Mike for accommodation etc., and both were even asked to stay for an extra day to go over to Macau to play a game of golf before returning to the UK. Magic.

On another occasion, in 1992 when Mike was studying at University in Edinburgh, an American naval officer from Chevron Shipping, attending a workshop in Birmingham run by David, asked about playing golf in Scotland for the bank-holiday weekend. So a deal was struck: he could meet Mike in Edinburgh and fund a weekend's golf – including the hallowed St Andrews Old Course – for the two of them, using Mike's car.

Mike at the time (and who had previously gained a B.Sc. in Biochemistry at Bangor University) was on his postgraduate malting and brewing course at Heriot-Watt University, Edinburgh, and like his dad became a fully qualified brewer that year.

David continued his management consultancy work until 2001 when he had reached the ripe old age of 60. As we shall now see, this did not stop him indulging in biking and sailing adventures before he retired...

Chapter Eleven

Gel and Our Kid start cycling again…

David and his school friend Gel had done a lot of cycling in their teens, going off for several days at a time to places like Cheddar Gorge and along the south coast and the Isle of Wight. Gel had stayed on at Birmingham University to complete a doctorate, had emigrated to America in the '60s, then later became the Professor of Oncology and Microbiology at the University of British Columbia, Vancouver, Canada. They had over the years kept in touch, meeting whenever Gel visited the UK to see his mother who lived in Bromsgrove.

In May 1996, he contacted David to suggest that they do some biking together. David was amazed – he hadn't owned a bike for decades. Nonetheless he agreed, as the pair of them by this time were only 55 years old and David's self-employed management consultancy activities allowed him plenty of freedom. So he bought a mountain bike, and started getting fit before Gel arrived, by biking a few canal towpaths, which of course are pretty numerous in the Midlands and which a few of them David had biked when we had lived all those years ago in Hockley. Not only that: from Day One he decided to record every trip, with pictures and maps.

Gel duly arrived and they spent a few days on the Birmingham and Worcester Canal plus a couple of weeks on the canal towpaths in Wales and up to Chester, before Gel returned to Vancouver.

The Guinness World Record…

Our Kid had loved biking those few canals with Gel, so he made the enormous mental leap of decided to bike all of the canal towpaths in England, and which later he extended to include Scotland and Ireland. That's what he did over the course of the next 18 months, a few days or a couple of weeks at a time, usually on his own but sometimes with his friends from his local pub, and including Gel

Gel and Our Kid at the Diglis Basin, Worcester.

coming back for more. By the end of this odyssey, he had covered 2,500 miles of towpath and had written a 200-page book, full of maps and pictures.

He couldn't get the book published because it would have been pretty boring to most people, and more importantly biking was not allowed on most of the towpaths so he'd been (typically?) a naughty boy. Undeterred, he sent one of his two precious copies (produced on his home printer) to the Chief Executive of British Waterways (which owned the vast majority of the canals) simply saying "Sir, look what I've gone and done, hope you don't send me to jail"; and to his amazement he received this reply: "Thanks for letting me have sight of the survey you have conducted of our waterways, I give you retrospective permission for having done so". What a man! What a sense of humour! So, now armed with an approved book, he sent it to Guinness World Records asking if he could be granted a Guinness World Record for biking all the extant towpaths of the canals

Chapter Eleven

GUINNESS
WORLD RECORDS

CERTIFICATE

ON 4 DECEMBER 1997, DAVID COX COMPLETED HIS CYCLING JOURNEY OF TRAVELLING THE EXTANT TOWPATHS OF GREAT BRITAIN AND IRELAND, A DISTANCE OF APPROXIMATELY 2500 MILES STARTING ON 1 JUNE 1996 AT CHESLYN HAY, STAFFORDSHIRE AND FINISHING IN NORTH WALSHAM, NORFOLK ON 4 DECEMBER 1997

Keeper of the Records
GUINNESS WORLD RECORDS

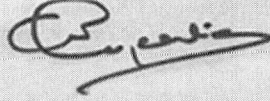

of Britain and Ireland. Six months later, another amazement: a certificate arrived in the post: he had been granted that Guinness World Record! It has to be his proudest personal achievement! And no, I don't know what Mom and Dad would have said about it, but I can guess.

I can't possibly include here a description of all the tales he told me of what adventures he had whilst doing all this biking. Suffice to say he only fell into a canal once, the Grand Union Canal near Rugby, with his bike plus camera, plus cigars.

More biking with Gel in France...

His biking with Gel hadn't finished. In 1999, both aged 58, they decided to bike a few of the French canals. The first was the Canal de Brest et Nantes in Brittany, some 200 miles long. That took two weeks, starting with a ferry ride to St Malo. They stayed in gites they came to each day, using their schoolboy French from Handsworth Grammar at each cafe and bar and restaurant, always seeking the cheapest of them as a challenge. Whenever they ate a meal they always chose something they couldn't translate: David remembers particularly once enjoying a plate of stewed whelks!

A year later, they went on their latest and final canal bike ride. They flew with their bikes to Bordeaux and biked from there, on the Atlantic coast, along the

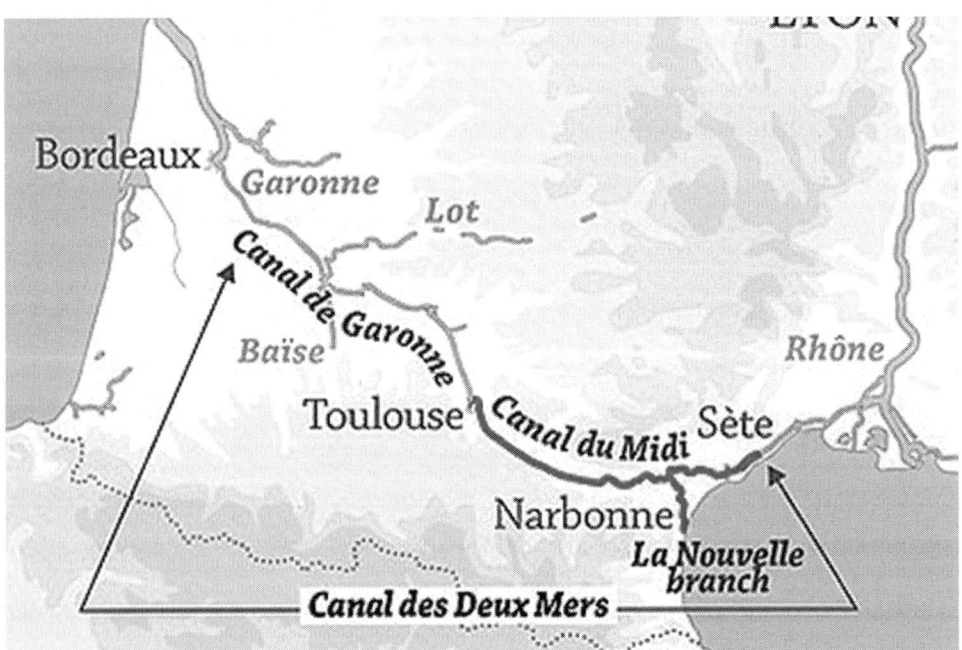

Chapter Eleven

navigable river Garonne to Toulouse. Then they continued on the Canal du Midi which took them down to Sete on the Mediterranean: that was the most memorable canal they had both ever biked along. Stunning. Then it was just a short ride for the two of them to Montpellier to catch the plane back home.

Our Kid becomes a sailor...

Overlapping at the time with biking in France, in 1998 he was invited by Dave Jolley, one of his friends from Brewing School days, to sail on his wife Debbie's 36 foot Rustler yacht to Ireland for a couple of weeks. Instead he stayed for six, ringing Peggy every week to check that she was still happy for him to stay with them. Of course she was! This voyage took them round the south coast of Ireland and up to Dingle Bay where they met Fungi, a dolphin that had taken up residence in the bay and had become a tourist attraction.

He had caught the sailing bug. Soon after that he went on a couple of training courses, the first on the south coast and the next in Gibraltar, and emerged highly qualified as a Coastal Skipper. (Mostly) via a website called Crewseekers, over the course of the next 10 – yes, 10 – years (and I've examined his official log book to check this): he crewed on more than 15 different yachts, and chartered a few more from Sunsail as skipper, and covered nearly 20,000 miles at sea (all on sail boats, never motorboats), including: two Atlantic crossings, several voyages in the Caribbean from Trinidad to the Virgin Isles, and several voyages in the Mediterranean including trips to Istanbul, Venice, Dubrovnik, Troy, Ephesus, Crete, Sicily, the Balearic Islands, Cannes, the Dalmatian Coast, up and down the coast of Turkey, and most of the Greek Islands . He could fill his own book with his sea-going tales, but here I'll just describe a few.

His most expensive meal ever: in 2001 at the Cotton Club on Mustique (made famous by Princess Margaret and Mick Jagger), £100, enjoyed as skipper with his crew friends from his local pub in Shenstone, Staffs, none of whom had sailed before, on a yacht chartered from Sunsail.

His cheapest week's stay ever: crewing on a yacht when they berthed in a private yacht club on the island of San Giorgio, Venice, overlooking St. Mark's Square – 42 Euros each, total for the week.

His most scary moment ever: during his first crossing of the Atlantic, at dawn when the light is confusing, in the middle of the ocean, and after more than two days of not having seen a single ship, a huge freighter appeared as if out of nowhere heading straight at them on a collision course and not responding to his skipper's radio warning (when it should have – despite its size, it has to give way to sail), and having to take immediate action to get out of its way.

His best yacht ever: Gigi, a 56 foot Oyster, the 'Rolls Royce' of yachts, on which he crewed on his second Atlantic crossing – here it is.

His best skipper and most intellectual powerhouse: Max Wilkinson, a retired deputy editor of the *Financial Times*, owner and skipper of the 41 foot Westerly Ocean Lord 'Poppy of Orwell' and for whom Our Kid crewed for more than three years including voyages up the Aegean to Istanbul, back around Greece, up the Adriatic to Venice and back down to the Ionian, Greece. Our Kid was appointed 'the ship's Bard' by Max on these many voyages, having discovered his hidden talent for writing poetry. Here's an example, written when leaving the yacht Poppy to overwinter in a boat yard, their basil plant having to be thrown away:

> Basil has served us quite well,
> He's made all our salads taste swell,
> But we're leaving Poppy,
> So he's for the choppy,
> It's goodbye, adieu and farewell.

How's that for talent!

And more sailing tales…

His worst skipper: a nameless Italian, who crashed his yacht on rocks along the Dalmatian Coast, and refused to have the damage inspected before sailing across to Italy, so Our Kid 'abandoned ship' and flew home.

His most obscenely expensive view of yachts ever: berthed in the marina of St. Martin, in the Caribbean, rows of huge 100-foot-plus motor boats and which included one of Abramovich's fleet.

Chapter Eleven

His most surprising beach: on the northern coast of St. Barts, in the Caribbean, which turned out to be crowded with nude bathers (and of course he joined in: took his kit off and had a swim).

His most enjoyable drinking session: after three nearly-alcohol-free weeks (on his first) crossing of the Atlantic, within minutes of docking in Nelson's dockyard, Antigua, meeting Jim the barman and enjoying rum punches, followed by 100 proof rum 'shots' straight out of the freezer, in the raging sunshine.

His biggest yacht: the 72 foot Whitbread, a ketch, with a crew of 12 plus owner and a skipper, the voyage being from Gosport to the Canary Isles.

His personally created disasters whilst sailing: none, he says!

His volcanic experience: he was on night watch when sailing from Syracruse, Sicily, heading for Malta. He developed really itchy eyes in the middle of the night, only to find when he awoke the next day that the yacht was covered in black volcanic dust, which had obviously irritated his eyes. Mount Etna had erupted! The dust cloud chased them all the way to the marina in Malta. When it had dispersed, all the crews started washing down their boats, which produced a comical sight: whilst there was enough water pressure for the motor boats, there was only enough to reach half way up the sail boats, which therefore continued to have black tops!

His failure as a snorkelling fisherman: in the Ionian, when all he caught over several days was a tiny octopus, not even large enough to cook and eat; and one little fish, superb as an hors d'oeuvre for one.

His non voyage: he flew to Trinidad to crew on a catamaran. He arrived to find that the young (ex public schoolboy) owner/skipper had met his other crew

member, a young attractive lady newly graduated from Oxford University, at Heathrow, had flown out with her a couple of days earlier, and by the time Our Kid arrived they had become 'an item'. So Our Kid was told he was surplus to requirements! So much for British values! So, he spent an enforced one-week holiday on Tobago and then flew home, much to Peggy's annoyance as she hadn't expected him back for possibly weeks!

His drugs trial: was on Jost Van Dyke Island in the British Virgins. There was a 'magic mushroom' party: it had no effect on him.

His steel drum band experience: this was at Shirley Heights, Antigua, a most amazing band (billed as the best in the Caribbean).

His sailing had to finish...

And so it was in August 2009, when David was 68 years old, that he enjoyed his last sailing adventure. He self-confessed to 'starting to creak', to feel that physically he was not able to be a fully participating crew member any more, let alone be in charge as a skipper.

Appropriately, his last voyage was with his long-term skipper Max on his yacht Poppy in the Ionian. He waved goodbye to both of them in Lefkas, Greece.

The apartment in Spain...

In 2004, aged 63, just three years after he had formally retired and was half way through his sailing adventures, he thought he might buy an apartment in Spain! At that time, his daughter Jane, now aged 36, had a boyfriend, Paul, who had just inherited a large sum of money, and he and David decided to buy such an apartment together as an investment.

Not only that, he bought a Vespa there! Well, a Piaggio – the same company – and a 250cc model at that, able to even overtake lorries on the motorways. He once even rode it back to his local – The Fox in Shenstone – and back to the apartment. And he even let me ride it, with Carole on the back. That brought back distant memories.

Paul and he enjoyed their investment (the apartment was in Empuriabrava, Catalonia), it made them some money, but for a variety of reasons they decided to sell it, which they did in 2014.

Chapter Twelve

And now...

David met Jill in Spain, and as a result in 2013, Peggy and he decided to separate. It has thankfully turned out to be as amicable as such an event can be. Peggy has bought her own cottage in Shenstone (the village where the family lived for 30 years), and Jill and David live south of Birmingham, in a cottage in Studley.

Meanwhile, David's daughter Jane remains unmarried, lives in Tamworth and breeds poodles; and Mike and Nic live in Boston Spa in Yorkshire. He is a brewer and she is a nurse, and they have a daughter Hannah. As Carole and I have no children, Hannah is the last of the Cox's.

Carole and I continue to live in Sutton Coldfield.

Forever brothers...

Me and Our Kid have always kept in touch, meet regularly and still love each other dearly. I think as we have got older we have developed a stronger bond than that formed out of our tragedy all those years ago when we lost our dear Mom and Dad.

Well dear brother I hope you have enjoyed this account of our life first presented to you for your sixtieth birthday, telling the story up to when you were 21, now extended to describe some of what we've done since then into our late seventies.

Love
Malcolm

*Granddad Coxy
and Hannah, 2012.*

Appendix

*Our Family Tree, our Relatives
and a few pics from our Family Album*

Appendix

Our Family Tree

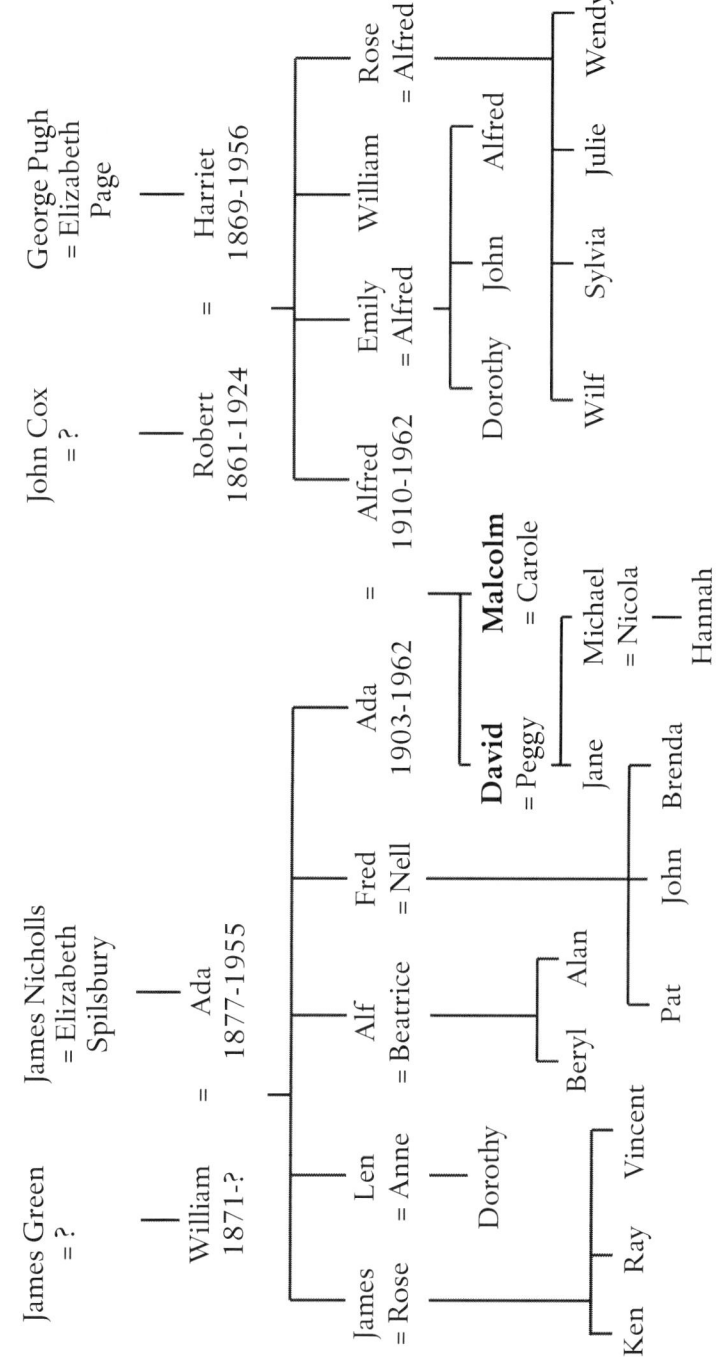

Our extended family...

Our Mom (Ada) was the only girl in her family and she had four brothers, Uncles Jim, Fred, Len and Alf in that order. Their mom and dad, our maternal granddad and grandmom, were William and Ada Green.

Alf and Fred used to come and see our Mom every Friday straight from work and have a sandwich and a cup of tea on their way home. It was our Mom who

Aunt Anne, Dorothy and Uncle Len.

Appendix

kept the family together and we had a whole range of male and female cousins who we used to see on high days and holidays.

Now my brother has always had a head like an empty bucket, so I have listed the family below. Mom was the eldest.

Uncle Len was married to Aunt Anne and had a daughter Dorothy.

Uncle Jim was married to Aunt Rose and had three children: Ken, Raymond, and Vincent.

Uncle Fred was married to Aunt Nell who had three children: Brenda, John and Pat.

Uncle Jim, Aunt Rose, Raymond, Ken and Vincent.

Uncle Alf was married to Aunt Beattie and had two children: Beryl and Alan.

Dad (Alf) had two sisters, Emily and Rose: he also had a brother Billy (William) who unfortunately died in his thirties from pneumonia.

Aunt Emily was the eldest and was married to Alf Rodgers and they had three children: Margaret, John and Alfred. Alf unfortunately died of leukaemia at the age of sixteen.

Aunt Rose was the younger sister and was married to Alf Ions (brother of Beattie who was married to Mom's brother, Alf). They had a son and three daughters, Wilf, Sylvia, Julie, and Wendy. I suppose that with sister and brother

Uncle Fred (left). Uncle Alf and Aunt Rose (right). Aunt Rose, Uncle Alf, Sylvia and Julie (far right).

Beryl and Alan.

Uncle Alf, Aunt Beattie and Mom.

marrying into both families, we are all first cousins.

Cousin Wilf went missing for a few years which me and Our Kid found very strange. It turned out he had held up a post office with his mate, his mate having a toy gun, resulting in them having a holiday in Winson Green nick.

Uncle Alf and Aunt Emily.

John and Margaret.

A couple of pics from our Family Album...

A night out in the '80s – Peggy, Me, Carole and David.

*The Cox Clan at the wedding of Mike and Nicola, 2008:
Me, Jane, David, Peggy, Carole, Nic and Mike.*

Appendix

And at Our Kid's 75th Birthday...

Jill with Elly Bunn.

Me and Carole.

School kids together: Nod Page, Our Kid (complete with his school cap) and Dave Bunn singing the Handsworth Grammar School song 'To the Old Bridge Trust'.

Me and Our Kid: forever brothers.